ANTALYA

POCKET TRAVEL GUIDE 2025

Experience the Magic of Antalya: History, Culture, Hidden Gems, Local Secrets, Culinary Delights and Essential Tips for an Unforgettable Journey – With Practical Guidance & Maps

BY

EDISON CLINE

TABLE OF CONTENTS

MY EXPERIENCE IN ANTALYA

My experience in Antalya was not merely a visit—it was a deep, almost transformative encounter with a place where history and hedonism co-exist under the embrace of the Mediterranean sun. As a seasoned traveler who's written guides across continents, I tend to approach each destination with a cautious optimism—keen to see if it lives up to its reputation. But Antalya didn't just meet expectations; it defied and surpassed them in the most unexpected ways. The moment my feet touched the warm stones of Kaleiçi, the city's ancient heart, I felt as if time had quietly folded in on itself, letting the whispers of centuries past wrap around me like silk. It began with a morning walk through the old town, where the cobbled lanes seemed to breathe stories. The scent of orange blossoms drifted through air that had both a salt-laced sharpness from the nearby sea and a stillness that hinted at an older, slower world. Kaleiçi is not polished for tourists; it's preserved like a memory that refuses to fade. The timber-framed Ottoman houses with their flower-boxed windows seemed to lean inward, as if sharing secrets. I lingered by the ancient Roman-era Hadrian's Gate, touching the weather-worn marble and thinking how emperors and merchants had once passed the same archway, with dreams not too different from my own.

One afternoon, I stood on the cliffs near Karaalioğlu Park, watching the vast sweep of the Mediterranean beneath me. The sea was impossibly blue—so vivid, it didn't look real. Just beyond, the jagged Taurus Mountains loomed, their snowy crowns glinting in the sun like silver helmets. There's something humbling about that view, something that silences even the most restless mind. And I say that as someone who doesn't stop moving often. Antalya taught me to slow down. I remember taking a dolmuş—those local shared minibuses—up into the highlands one day. I wanted to explore Termessos, the ruins of a city set high in the mountains, hidden away like a forgotten poem. Climbing through that ghostly city, where stone theatres and colonnades sat beneath pine trees and tangled vines, I realized I wasn't alone. The silence was so complete that every gust of wind felt like a voice from another time. I sat in the ancient amphitheatre and watched eagles fly overhead, not another soul in sight. That kind of solitude—ancient, sacred, and earned—is rare in our world. Antalya still offers it, if you're willing to seek it.

But the city isn't just for quiet reflection. The nights, particularly in the harbour district, are alive with music and laughter. I dined at a modest family-run meyhane, where the meze came in endless waves and the raki flowed as if it were part of some unspoken ritual. The owner's son, who couldn't have been more than twelve, played the saz with surprising soul, and I sat among strangers who quickly became companions. Time expanded there, between the clinking of glasses and the rhythm of old Turkish songs echoing into the sea breeze. It's hard to explain the emotional hold Antalya has without sounding overly poetic, but perhaps that's the point. It isn't a place you simply see—it's one you feel. I've walked through Petra, climbed Machu Picchu, and wandered the alleys of Kyoto, but there's a certain intimacy in Antalya that's different. Maybe it's the way the past doesn't shoutbut gently nudges you. Maybe it's how the locals live not to impress, but to share. Or maybe it's just how the sea seems to follow you, whether you're on the beach at Konyaaltı or sipping tea on a rooftop terrace.

I left Antalya reluctantly, as though pulling away from a friend mid-conversation. And even now, months later, there are moments when I close my eyes and find myself back in that narrow alley off Hesapçı Sokak, where the shadows are long, the air smells of jasmine and grilled eggplant, and the call to prayer hangs in the golden dusk like a sacred lullaby. I've travelled widely, and I'll continue to do so, but Antalya has lodged itself somewhere deeper in my soul—a place of quiet marvels and enduring warmth. If ever there was a place that blended myth and moment, that held both your heart and your senses in equal measure, it is Antalya. And should you ever go, go with time in your pocket and wonder in your eyes, because Antalya will meet you not as a destination, but as a story still being written.

BENEFITS OF THIS GUIDE

Stepping into Antalya, one feels the pulse of a city that fuses ancient elegance with Mediterranean vivacity. This comprehensive guide is not just a publication, it is a curated passport to the city's soul. Compact yet comprehensive, this guide distills a lifetime of travel insight into a digestible and visually inviting companion. With up-to-date entries, readers benefit from real-time awareness of opening hours, seasonal changes, and cultural nuances.

Maps and Navigation
The guide includes detailed, hand-drawn maps of Old Town (Kaleiçi), beaches, ruins, and hiking trails. These aren't generic GPS downloads but thoughtfully illustrated layouts with walking distances, elevation cues, and landmark orientation. With it in your hand, getting lost in Antalya becomes a joy instead of a frustration.

Accommodation Options
Each listing includes authentic reviews, price ranges, and insider tips on securing the best rooms. It even covers pet-friendly spots, solo traveler preferences, and accessibility features often missed elsewhere.

Transportation
This guide makes navigating Antalya's transport ecosystem both easy and economical. It explains local buses, tram lines, dolmuş systems, and taxi etiquette, with fare estimates and route times. Airport transfers, car rentals, and even electric scooter spots are clearly outlined for seamless movement.

Top Attractions
From the marble columns of Hadrian's Gate to the theatre of Aspendos, the guide highlights each site's cultural weight. It doesn't just say what to see—it explains why it matters, when to go, and how to experience it without the crowds. It also introduces offbeat attractions rarely found in mainstream travel books.

Practical Information and Travel Resources
Visa rules, currency exchanges, emergency contacts, and local customs are laid out in a no-nonsense format. There are guides on tipping practices, dress codes, religious sensitivities, and even how to handle minor medical needs. QR codes also lead to live embassy info and weather updates.

Culinary Delights

This guide captures Antalya's edible heritage, from sizzling kebabs to humble gözleme cooked by elderly village women. It shares which eateries locals love, how to spot authentic meze spreads, and why coastal fish shacks often outshine formal restaurants. Even street food is decoded, down to sauces and preparation methods.

Culture and Heritage

Antalya's historical layers are woven with Roman, Seljuk, and Ottoman threads, all traced clearly in this guide. It connects each monument, mosque, and museum to its historical context and present significance. There's also commentary on cultural performances, religious festivals, and community values.

Outdoor Activities and Adventures

The guide leads adventurers to Antalya's best hiking paths, including the Lycian Way and Taurus Mountains. It covers paragliding, canyoning, diving, and even hot-air ballooning nearby—with safety notes, prices, and booking links. Each experience is reviewed with authenticity and realistic expectations.

Shopping

Handcrafted leather goods, locally woven kilims, and signature Turkish delights are described in detail. Bargaining tips, authenticity checks, and shipping advice are included for peace of mind.

Day Trips and Excursions

Antalya's surroundings are a trove of day-trip gems, from the ruins of Perge to the waterfalls of Düden. The guide offers itineraries, bus timings, private car rental tips, and what to expect at each destination. Each day trip balances activity with relaxation, giving options for all travel styles.

Entertainment and Nightlife

From chic rooftop lounges to traditional Turkish taverns with live saz music, Antalya's nightlife is multilayered. The guide lays out which areas suit jazz lovers, where students gather, and which venues stay open till dawn. Cultural shows, belly-dancing performances, and sunset cruises are also spotlighted.

CHAPTER 1
INTRODUCTION TO ANTALYA

1.1 Welcome to Antalya

Welcome to Antalya—a city that doesn't just sit on the Mediterranean coast, it owns it. There's something about arriving here that makes the heart stir in ways you weren't quite expecting. Maybe it's the scent of salt in the air mingled with the sweetness of citrus groves, or the way the light lingers over the Taurus Mountains before it falls into the sea. Whatever it is, Antalya has a strange power to feel familiar even if it's your first time. It offers more than a destination. It offers a state of mind—one that's relaxed, warm, and deeply ancient. Stepping into Antalya is like turning the page of a long-lost storybook where every corner writes its own tale. The city is alive with voices from centuries past. Roman emperors once walked here, Ottoman traders exchanged silk and spice, and the early Anatolian people left behind mysterious ruins that whisper in the wind.

Modern life has unfolded around these remnants of history, not burying them but embracing them. This seamless blend of time gives the city its soul—a sense that the past has never really left, just made room for the present to flourish beside it. There is something humbling about walking the old harbour as fishing boats sway gently with the tide, their wooden hulls groaning softly as if remembering stories of storms and sunshine. Beyond the marina, the streets spill out in every direction, each one holding a promise. A tiny tea shop where old men play backgammon under the shade of a fig tree, a quiet art gallery tucked behind an unassuming archway, the faint call to prayer rising and falling like breath itself. These aren't curated experiences—they are lived ones. Antalya does not dress itself up for tourists. It is what it is. That honesty is part of its charm.

The heartbeat of the city is its people. They are warm, direct, and proud—rightly so. They do not rush life; they greet it each day like a trusted friend. Conversations are long, laughter is generous, and hospitality is not an act, it is a habit. It's the kind of place where you sit for coffee and end up staying for dinner, where a stranger might point you in the right direction and walk half the way with you. This sincerity is what leaves a lasting imprint. Long after the beauty of the beaches fades from memory, the kindness of the people remains vivid. There is a certain rhythm to Antalya's days that makes you forget the clock. Mornings begin softly with the sound of seagulls and the clink of breakfast being laid out on balconies. Midday sun sharpens the sea into a mirror of turquoise, calling swimmers and sunbathers to its edge. By late afternoon, a golden hush falls over the land, the heat easing into a slow, warm breath. And then come the evenings—calm, fragrant, and glowing with lights from cafes, gardens, and rooftop terraces where friends and strangers come together under the same starlit sky. Each day has its own texture, its own way of unwinding, as if the city wants you to unlearn stress and relearn stillness.

To describe Antalya only in terms of landscapes or weather is to miss the point. Yes, the sea is blue, and the cliffs are dramatic, and the sun seems to shine longer than it should—but the real draw is something less obvious. It's in the silences between conversations, in the stillness of a side street at dusk, in the way even the wind seems to pause when it passes over ancient stone. It's in the sense of belonging you feel not because you're from here, but because the city invites you in without question. You don't visit Antalya to tick it off a list. You come here to be reminded of something you might have forgotten: how it feels to slow down, to savour, to connect without needing a reason. You come here not just to see new places, but to feel something real again—something that perhaps only a place like this can awaken in you. And when it's finally time to leave, as it always is, you won't say goodbye in the usual way. You'll carry

Antalya with you—in your senses, in your stories, in the part of you that knows something rare has just happened. Something you didn't expect. Something you will return to, if not in person, then always in memory.

1.2 History and Culture

Antalya carries the weight of empires, civilizations, and centuries of human experience etched into every stone and ruin. This city is not a product of modern tourism—it is an heirloom of Anatolia's deep past, a living remnant of layered history that continues to shape its present identity. To understand Antalya is to look beyond its scenic coastlines and delve into its soul, formed over thousands of years through the convergence of East and West. The spirit of the city is not frozen in time but continues to evolve with a deep reverence for its ancient heartbeat.

From Attalos II to the Roman Touch

The city owes its founding to Attalos II, a king of Pergamon who, around the second century BCE, ordered his men to discover "heaven on earth," and upon their return, Antalya—then Attaleia—was established. This move positioned the city as a key maritime gateway on the Mediterranean. It thrived under Roman rule, gaining the status of a major port where emperors like Hadrian left behind architectural marks, the most enduring of which is Hadrian's Gate. These centuries laid a strong classical foundation, not only in stone and engineering but in the civic culture that valued urban life, education, and connection to the greater Roman world. The city became a melting pot of pagan rituals and early Christian growth, offering a glimpse into the religious transition of the Mediterranean.

Byzantine and Seljuk Influence

Following the fall of the Western Roman Empire, Antalya transitioned into the Byzantine fold, where Christianity firmly took root, turning the city into a bastion of Orthodox belief. Churches emerged, and religious life dominated public rhythm, supported by monastic communities tucked into the region's rugged terrain. The Seljuks arrived in the 13th century and infused the city with Islamic character while retaining respect for existing traditions. They repaired, expanded, and transformed the skyline with madrasas, mosques, and caravanserais that still whisper the stories of their time. The Yivli Minaret, an enduring symbol of Seljuk craftsmanship, marked Antalya's cultural pivot as

East began to meet West not through conflict, but through a cultural coexistence that shaped its architectural and spiritual language.

Ottoman Continuity and Transition

Under Ottoman rule, Antalya found a sense of continuity rather than abrupt change. The Ottomans allowed the city to grow at its own rhythm while preserving its multicultural roots. The old town—Kaleiçi—took its current form during this period, with winding alleys, timber-framed houses, and the interweaving of mosques and market stalls. Cultural life was anchored in community gatherings, seasonal festivals, and the rhythm of maritime trade. Antalya during this era was a meeting ground for Greeks, Turks, Armenians, and Jews, living in a shared social fabric that emphasized mutual reliance despite ethnic and religious distinctions. It was neither just a village nor a capital, but something in between—steadfast in tradition, and modest in expression, yet rich in cultural layering.

Cultural Identity and Folk Traditions

The cultural fabric of Antalya draws its strength from the quiet but powerful traditions passed down through generations. Music, dance, and oral storytelling remain central, with the Teke region's distinct rhythms and shadow puppet plays maintaining their hold in rural areas. Weddings, harvest celebrations, and circumcision feasts are not only private affairs but public spectacles that reaffirm community identity. Cuisine is steeped in age-old practices—grape molasses, tahini, and sun-dried tomatoes speak of subsistence and creativity born from the land. The city's cultural memory is held not just in monuments, but in the way tea is poured, how carpets are woven, and how the past is acknowledged in every gesture, often without the need for explanation.

Historical Monuments as Living Testaments

Antalya's monuments are more than attractions—they are memory stones that preserve the layers of its historical consciousness. The ancient theatre in Aspendos continues to echo performances two millennia later, not out of nostalgia but from reverence to enduring artistry. Perge's colonnaded streets and Hellenistic gates are not fenced relics but open pages in the city's evolving narrative. The Antalya Museum does more than display—it teaches continuity, where statues and artifacts are placed not behind glass but within reach of understanding. These sites are not frozen in the past; they speak to a culture that never saw history as something to be admired from afar but as something to be lived with, reflected upon, and cherished in the marrow of daily life.

1.3 Geography and Climate

Antalya, located on the southwestern coast of Turkey along the Gulf of Antalya, is a region where the sea meets the rugged Taurus Mountains in a dramatic embrace. This city stands as a geographical marvel, attracting visitors with its unique blend of coastline, cliffs, rivers, and fertile plains. Every turn of the road reveals a contrast between modern development and ancient terrain that has shaped civilizations for millennia. This is a land defined by contours, carved by weather and time.

Mediterranean Coastal Zone

Antalya's defining geographical character is its broad sweep of Mediterranean coastline, marked by long beaches, rocky promontories, and clear blue waters that stretch endlessly to the horizon. The beaches of Konyaaltı and Lara lie just minutes from the heart of the city, offering easy access for those staying in central Antalya. Konyaaltı Beach runs along the western flank of the city beneath the towering cliffs, while Lara, located southeast around 12 kilometers away, features soft sands that give way to the warm turquoise sea. These areas host the rhythmic life of the coast and capture the heart of summer.

The Taurus Mountain Barrier

The Taurus Mountains rise sharply behind the city, forming an imposing barrier that defines both the visual landscape and the regional climate. These mountains are not merely scenic—they act as a weather shield, separating the coast from the harsher interior of Anatolia. Reaching heights above 3,000 meters, they feed rivers like the Düden and Köprülü that cascade toward the sea. The mountains also create opportunities for outdoor pursuits, particularly around Saklıkent, just 50 kilometers from central Antalya, where winter skiing meets summer hiking. Their presence lends a grandeur to the horizon and a crispness to the air.

River Valleys and Fertile Plains

The area around Antalya is fed by a network of rivers and underground springs that water fertile plains like the Aksu and Serik lowlands. These plains are key to the city's agricultural economy, yielding citrus fruits, olives, and pomegranates in abundance. The Düden River, with its dramatic waterfalls both inland and along the coastal cliffs, flows directly through the urban environment, becoming part of the daily scenery. These green corridors soften the built landscape and hint at the region's agricultural richness, which has long supported settlements from the ancient Pamphylian cities to the modern metropolis.

Climate and Seasonal Variations

In Antalya, July and August bring temperatures above 34°C, with sunlight from early morning till late evening. Winter months like January rarely see temperatures dip below 10°C, and rainfall is common from December through March. Spring, particularly April and May, and autumn months such as late September and October provide a pleasant balance, with moderate heat and lower humidity. The sea remains warm from May to October, making it ideal for swimming, even outside the peak summer months, which can often feel oppressive for inland exploration.

Best Time to Visit Antalya

The most rewarding time to visit Antalya is during the shoulder seasons of late spring and early autumn when the air is comfortable and the crowds are thinner. From mid-April to early June, the landscape is alive with blooming flora, and coastal breezes temper the rising heat. September and October offer warm sea temperatures with fewer tourists, making excursions to historical sites like Termessos or Perge more enjoyable. These months allow visitors to fully appreciate the layered geography of the region, from the pine-clad hills to the sweeping coves of the coast, without the extremes of weather or mass tourism.

1.4 Antalya for First Time Travelers

Antalya is more than a resort city. It is a place where the call of the sea meets the stories carved into ancient stones. To walk its streets is to brush shoulders with centuries of history while the sun burns gently on your skin and the scent of the Mediterranean carries through the air.

Getting To Know Antalya

Antalya is located on the southwestern coast of Turkey, directly facing the turquoise waters of the Mediterranean Sea. It lies within the province of the same name and serves as its capital, forming a major part of the Turkish Riviera. Its position makes it both a historic maritime hub and a modern resort escape. The city is bordered by the Beydağları Mountains to the west and the fertile plains of Pamphylia to the east. It is well connected through Antalya Airport, about 13 kilometres northeast of the city centre, linking it efficiently to both European capitals and domestic cities.

The Old Town Experience
Kaleiçi, Antalya's historic centre, is the heart where time slows down and the rhythm of daily life runs close to its roots. Surrounded by ancient Roman walls, it is a compact area that carries memories from Roman, Byzantine, Seljuk and Ottoman rule. The streets coil around key landmarks like Hadrian's Gate, an archway built in 130 AD to honour the Roman Emperor's visit. Within walking distance is the Yivli Minaret Mosque, a structure with its distinctive fluted minaret rising above the town. This part of Antalya is also home to boutique hotels, traditional Turkish bathhouses and local markets that make it a central starting point for any first-time visitor.

Climate And What To Expect
Antalya is blessed with a Mediterranean climate, meaning hot, dry summers and mild, rainy winters. The months from late April to October are best for beach holidays and outdoor exploration. July and August can be intensely warm, with temperatures often crossing 35°C, though the sea breeze from the Mediterranean offers some relief. Spring and autumn are ideal for sightseeing, especially if your interest leans toward ancient ruins or mountain trails. Rain is rare during the summer, but winter showers make the surrounding landscape burst into greenery and wildflowers. First-time visitors should come prepared for bright sunlight and hydration during summer months.

Places That Deserve Your Time
The region offers far more than beach resorts. Aspendos, located about 45 kilometres east of the city, is one of the best-preserved Roman theatres in the world, still hosting concerts under the open sky.. The Düden Waterfalls, both upper and lower falls, are easy day trips within the Antalya urban area. Meanwhile, the Antalya Museum, on Konyaaltı Caddesi, stands as a powerful introduction to the region's deep archaeological and ethnographic heritage.

Local Life And Cultural Rhythm
While the coast thrives on tourism, the inner neighbourhoods reflect the slower pace of daily Turkish life. Tea houses fill with conversation in the mornings, and call to prayer punctuates the rhythm of the day. The food, heavily based on olive oil, lamb, and fresh vegetables, is an honest reflection of its Mediterranean ties.

Traditional music, handwoven textiles, and seasonal festivals offer a glimpse into a culture that is deeply proud yet warmly welcoming. Turkish hospitality is sincere, and first-time visitors often find themselves invited for tea, stories, and smiles.

Final Word For First Timers

Antalya is a place that grows on you not just through sights, but through its sensations—heat on your skin, the texture of ancient stone, the rhythm of lapping waves, the aroma of fresh bread in the market, and the sound of languages blending. It is a destination that welcomes curiosity with open arms. For those who step in with open eyes and patience to understand, Antalya does not simply reveal its beauty—it lets you live it. Your first trip will not be your last. The memory of Antalya lingers far longer than the duration of your stay.

CHAPTER 2
ACCOMMODATION OPTIONS

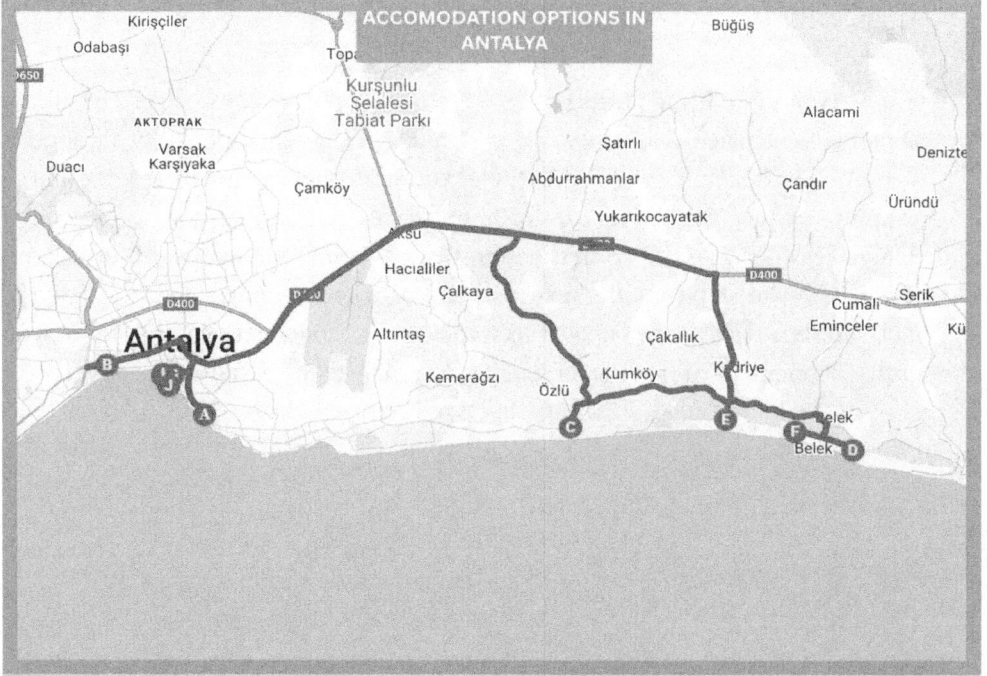

Directions from Akra Antalya, Şirinyalı, Lara Street, Muratpaşa/Antalya, Turkey to in the middle hotel, Gençlik, 1312. Sk., Muratpaşa/Antalya, Turkey

A
Akra Antalya, Sirinyalı, Lara Street, Muratpaşa/Antalya, Türkiye

B
Rixos Downtown Antalya, Meltem, Sakıp Sabancı Boulevard, Muratpaşa/Antalya, Türkiye

C
Titanic Mardan Palace, Ozlu, Aksu/Antalya, Türkiye

D
Maxx Royal Belek Golf Resort, Belek, Iskele Street, Serik/Antalya, Türkiye

E
Regnum Carya Golf & Spa Resort, Kadriye, Serik/Antalya, Türkiye

F
Susesi Luxury Resort, Belek, Serik/Antalya, Türkiye

G
Oscar Boutique Hotel, Haşimişcan, 1302. Sokak, Muratpaşa/Antalya, Türkiye

H
Hotel Blue Sea Garden, Kilincarslan, Hesapci Street, Muratpasa/Antalya, Türkiye

I
Hadrianus Hotel Kaleiçi, Kilincarslan, Zeytin Street, Muratpasa/Antalya, Türkiye

J
in the middle hotel, Gençlik, 1312. Sk., Muratpaşa/Antalya, Türkiye

2.1 Luxury Hotels and Resorts

Antalya's coast offers a selection of high-end hotels and resorts that seamlessly blend the warmth of traditional Turkish hospitality with cutting-edge facilities. These distinguished venues deliver refined service, gourmet dining, and curated cultural engagements. Each resort offers direct access to its official booking website, ensuring secure reservations and current availability.

Akra Antalya

Located at Lara Yolu in Muratpaşa, Akra Antalya is a five-star seafront retreat boasting sweeping views of the Mediterranean and the Bey Mountains. Guests can reserve rooms and suites via www.akrahotels.com/en/hotels/akra-antalya, with third-party rates starting around $118 per night. The property features five pools (including an infinity pool), a private Blue Flag beach, a full-service spa, and multiple dining venues from casual bistro to upscale rooftop restaurant. The hotel brings local culture to life through events like the jazz festival and urban-lounge experiences, along with bike tours. Combining modern convenience with time-honored hospitality, Akra is ideal for both business travelers and vacationers.

Rixos Downtown Antalya

Positioned on Sakıp Sabancı Boulevard in Meltem, Rixos Downtown Antalya offers an all-inclusive urban resort experience. Bookings are available at www.rixos.com/en/hotel-resort/rixos-downtown-antalya-land-legends-access, with deluxe rooms averaging about $247 per night. It has two outdoor pools, tennis courts, a cutting-edge fitness center, private black-sand beach with complimentary cabanas, and seven diverse restaurants. Guests enjoy MedWorld Health & Rehabilitation Center, an on-site golf driving range, and panoramic cocktails at the Rixos Lounge Bar. Perfectly located near Konyaaltı Beach and historic sites like Hadrian's Gate, it blends city exploration with resort luxury.

Titanic Mardan Palace

Titanic Mardan Palace graces Kundu in Aksu as an opulent garden-surrounded resort with its own beach. Reservations through www.titanic.com.tr/titanic-mardan-palace include Royal Duplex Suites from around €180 per night, while its King Suite can reach €6,000 nightly. Guests choose from lavish room types, including swim-up and lake houses, offering amenities such as private butlers, high-speed Wi-Fi, and Jacuzzi baths. On-site, you'll find the Amon Spa, multiple gourmet restaurants, expansive pools, and a children's club. Architectural grandeur with Greco-Roman influences, personalized guest service, and grand event venues define its luxurious character.

Maxx Royal Belek Golf Resort

Situated in Belek adjacent to PGA Sultan Golf Course, Maxx Royal Belek Golf Resort provides an Ultra All-Inclusive experience. Available at www.maxxroyal.com/belek-golf-resort, standard rooms start at US$317 per night, while luxury villas may exceed $1,600. The resort features butler services, Maxx Wellbeing Spa, multiple golf courses, and a private marina offering helicopter tours. Dining spans from Michelin-collaboration to themed beach bars, with family-oriented programming for children and evening entertainment for adults. The property's eco-conscious initiatives and global partnerships showcase its blend of durability, tradition, and innovation.

Regnum Carya Golf & Spa Resort

Located in Kadriye, Belek amidst pine forests and a championship golf course, Regnum Carya features an Ultra All-Inclusive model. Book via www.regnumhotels.com/RegnumCarya, with deluxe rooms from approximately $351 per night; villas and Crown Villas cost more. The resort offers ten à la carte restaurants, extensive spa and wellness facilities with hammam and hydrotherapy, indoor and outdoor pools, and a private sandy beach. Evening entertainment includes shows at an outdoor theater, plus rooftop infinity-pool lounging and night-lit tennis courts. Signature Crown Villa pool suites and full butler service blend traditional Turkish warmth with luxurious finishes.

Susesi Luxury Resort

Set in Belek on İskele Mevkii, Susesi Luxury Resort invites guests to its lakeside and beach surroundings. Reservations are available at www.susesihotel.com/en, with standard room rates beginning around $368 and private villa options at higher tiers. The spa—La Calisse—delivers bespoke treatments in serene surroundings, while seven specialty restaurants and elegant bars serve live music. Guests can make use of the resort's convention facilities, water sports, children's clubs, and nightly events..

2.2 Budget-Friendly Options

In the bustling core of Antalya, travelers on a budget can still discover accommodations that combine personality and practicality. Whether it's cozy guest houses in Kaleiçi's winding alleys or sleek boutique stays with Mediterranean views, these spots show that affordability and quality can go hand in hand. Each one offers its own charm, essential facilities, and close proximity to major attractions—all while keeping prices friendly for explorers wanting to spend more on experiences.

Oscar Boutique Hotel

Oscar Boutique Hotel stands out for its intimate atmosphere and attentive service, offering just 26 rooms surrounding a bright courtyard. You can reserve directly at www.hotel-oscar-antalya.h-rez.com. Situated at Atatürk Cad. 1302 Sok. No:12 in Kaleiçi's Old Town, this spot is both central and serene. Rooms start at around $48 per night, according to recent search listings. Complimentary Wi-Fi, air-conditioning, and on-site dining ensure a smooth stay, while its short walk to Hadrian's Gate and the historic marina keeps you connected to Antalya's iconic heritage.

Blue Sea Garden Hotel

Hesapci Sok. No:65, Blue Sea Garden Hotel surrounds guests with a courtyard garden and just 16 air-conditioned rooms. Bookings are available at www.blue-sea-garden.hotelsantalyaturkey.net/en/. Nightly rates begin at approximately $28, rarely exceeding $84. The hotel offers a complimentary buffet breakfast, an outdoor pool, bar/lounge, and free Wi-Fi throughout. Its relaxed, family-run ambiance delivers traditional Turkish hospitality steps from Mermerli Beach.

Hadrianus Pansion Hotel

Hadrianus Pansion feels boutique and contemporary, with only eight rooms—some featuring marble flooring and fireplaces. Located at Kılıçaslan Mahallesi, Zeytin Street, No:4 A/B, and bookable via www.hadrianus-hotel.antalyahotel.org/en/, this hotel offers nightly rates between $51 and $84, including breakfast. Positioned a short stroll from Hadrian's Gate and the clock tower, the tranquil garden offers a peaceful contrast to the lively city.

In The Middle Hotel

In The Middle Hotel blends art-deco design with modern comforts across its 13-room boutique layout. Situated at 1312. Sokak No:15 and bookable at www.inthemiddle.com.tr/, summer rates start at about £73.54 (~$92). Guests enjoy buffet breakfast, free in-room Wi-Fi, an in-house winery, and a rooftop terrace. With stylish décor and a location just five minutes from Mermerli Beach and the Old Bazaar, it appeals to travelers seeking both flair and convenience.

Hotel 1207 Special Class

Hotel 1207 Special Class spans two linked historic mansions on Barbaros Mahallesi Kocatepe Sokak No:13 in Kaleiçi. Reservations can be made through www.hotel1207.com. At roughly $56 per night—about $30 less than many local 3-star properties—it features a seasonal outdoor pool, library, garden courtyard, and complimentary breakfast. The combination of Ottoman architecture and contemporary amenities provides a comfortable yet memorable retreat.

Aspen Hotel

Hidden within Kaleiçi's labyrinthine lanes, Aspen Hotel centers around a peaceful pool and terrace café complete with a fireplace. You can reserve rooms via www.aspenhotel.com.tr/. With nightly rates from about $28 according to recent data, it's a standout for budget travelers. Amenities include free Wi-Fi, air-conditioning, a courtyard pool, rooftop terrace, and cozy lounge with garden views. Its convenient access to Mermerli Beach and the charming old town lanes ensures a memorable stay steeped in history.

2.3 Vacation Rentals and Apartments

Antalya continues to draw global travelers not just for its beaches and history, but for the modern, flexible accommodation choices it offers beyond traditional hotels. Vacation rentals and serviced apartments have gained significant appeal, particularly among visitors who want autonomy, extra space, and access to homely comforts during their stay. Spread across key locations such as Konyaaltı, Muratpaşa, Lara, and the broader Antalya Province including Side and Kemer, these apartments blend convenience with personal privacy.

Nox Suite Hotel

Found at Çağlayan Mahallesi 2015 Sokak No: 23 in Muratpaşa, Nox Suite Hotel offers stylish one-bedroom suites and spacious three-bedroom duplex apartments, each equipped with a private kitchenette, balcony, and blackout drapes for quiet evenings. Free Wi-Fi, an outdoor seasonal pool, and private parking enhance comfort, while thoughtful interior design gives the units a clean, modern atmosphere. The current starting rate is around $98 per night depending on booking season and room type. This property is especially convenient for those wanting both access to the coast and the city's dining options. Visit www.noxsuite.com/en/ for direct reservations.

Oli Hotel And Suites

Positioned at 616. Sokak No:13 in the Arapsuyu area of Konyaaltı, Oli Hotel and Suites offers a contemporary stay with studio and one-bedroom layouts. Each unit features a smart TV, kitchenette, and rainfall shower, along with complimentary Wi-Fi and 24-hour reception support. Prices begin around $87 per night for two adults, and the property is only a few minutes from the beach and the city's main sports venue. This apartment hotel caters well to couples and solo travelers who value minimalism with easy transport links. To secure a booking, head to oli-and-suites.antalyahotel.org/en/.

Antalya Suites Residences

Just moments away from Antalya's old city quarter of Kaleiçi, AntalyaSuites Residences presents a selection of bright studio and one-bedroom apartments designed for both short and long stays. Located centrally, these residences provide open-plan kitchens, full bathrooms, and balconies in many of the units, with prices beginning at approximately $82 per night. Secure parking and seamless check-in systems make it a practical choice for independent travelers. Those looking for a location that blends city life with beach access will find this appealing. For bookings, visit antalyasuites.com/.

Minta Apart Hotel

Minta Apart Hotel is a complex that includes practical apartments that feature kitchenettes, balconies, and air-conditioning, ideal for families or long-term guests. Wi-Fi is available throughout, and there's a reception team on hand around the clock. The average rate begins near $49 per night depending on room type and availability. Surrounded by beach life and local eateries, it's a solid choice for travelers seeking low-cost comfort. Book through www.mintaapart.net/.

Melissa Garden Apart Hotel

Set within the greater Manavgat region, Melissa Garden Apart Hotel places guests close to both ancient Roman ruins and modern beach facilities. Units here range from simple studios to more spacious one-bedroom apartments, all featuring kitchenettes, small patios, and garden access. The average nightly price stands near $60, with further discounts often available for weekly bookings. The property also provides Wi-Fi, on-site parking, and a calm, casual environment. This setting is particularly attractive to travelers combining historical interests with relaxation. Visit melissagardenhotel.com/ to confirm availability.

Lara Marine Homes

Situated in the Guzeloba neighborhood of Muratpaşa, Lara Marine Homes features self-contained apartments within easy reach of Lara Beach and TerraCity Mall. The accommodations include fully equipped kitchens, separate seating areas, and Wi-Fi, while the complex offers private parking and a swimming pool. Rates begin from approximately $67 per night, making it accessible for both short-term stays and seasonal visitors. Only a few kilometers from Antalya Airport, this rental is suited to guests looking for peaceful surroundings close to key transport routes. Visit www.laramarinehomes.com/ for bookings and full details.

2.4 Beachfront Properties

Antalya's coastline continues to draw global attention for its seamless blend of comfort, relaxation, and direct sea access. Travelers seeking a stay where the beach lies just beyond their doorstep will find a compelling mix of accommodation in the region. From Lara's luxury-heavy stretches to the more cosmopolitan shores of Konyaaltı, each property presents its own identity and character. These beachfront hotels not only guarantee panoramic views but also deliver top-tier amenities, fine dining, and direct booking access.

Akra Antalya

Akra Antalya is positioned at Şirinyalı, Lara Caddesi No: 24, 07100 Muratpaşa, Antalya, placing visitors directly above the Mediterranean cliffs. Rates begin near $58 per night, offering standard rooms with modern interiors and increasing with deluxe sea-facing upgrades. Guests can access several swimming pools, a full-service wellness center, and multiple restaurants with both indoor and outdoor seating. The man-made beach platform allows for a seaside experience despite its cliffside position, paired with views over the Beydağları range. Further details and reservations are handled through their official page: www.akrahotels.com/en/hotels/akra-antalya.

Titanic Deluxe Lara

Located at Yaşar Sobutay Bulvarı No:36, Lara, Antalya, Titanic Deluxe Lara places you on one of the city's longest private stretches of sand. Pricing typically starts around $110 per night, structured as all-inclusive, giving guests access to a wide range of food, drinks, and services. The resort is equipped with extensive water-based facilities, including a small on-site water park, indoor and outdoor pools, and a sports complex. It also offers spa services, multiple restaurants, and activity zones for both adults and children, functioning as a comprehensive resort village. Bookings and seasonal offers are available at www.titanic.com.tr/titanic-deluxe-lara.

Titanic Mardan Palace

Found at Kundu Mahallesi, Yaşar Sobutay Boulevard No:450/1, Aksu, Antalya, this property is often recognized for its opulent design and grand scale. Standard prices for rooms begin around $246 per night, with expansive suites and premium services available at significantly higher rates. The hotel features one of the largest outdoor pools in Europe, with lavish interiors, palatial décor, and a beach lined with private cabanas. With themed restaurants, a 24-hour concierge, Turkish spa experiences, and curated entertainment, it rivals the world's top beach resorts. For reservations, visit their booking platform directly at www.titanic.com.tr/tr/titanic-mardan-palace.

Rixos Downtown Antalya

Rixos Downtown Antalya, found at Sakıp Sabancı Boulevard No:3, Meltem, Muratpaşa, 07030 Antalya, combines beach access with an urban resort feel. Room rates start from $183 nightly, including access to Aruna Beach and entry to Land of Legends theme park through affiliated guest programs. Its facilities include panoramic elevators to the shore, open-air swimming pools, sports courts, and a dedicated wellness and spa complex. The location is ideal for travelers who prefer city amenities without sacrificing the convenience of beachfront leisure. More information and booking options can be found at www.rixos.com/en/hotel-resort/rixos-downtown-antalya-land-legends-access.

Lara Barut Collection

Set along Yasar Sobutay Boulevard No:30, Lara, Antalya, Lara Barut Collection delivers a large-scale beach resort experience with modern luxury. Pricing begins at approximately $361 per night under an ultra-all-inclusive model, which covers premium drinks and all on-site dining. The resort operates across over 130,000 square meters and features high-end amenities, gourmet restaurants, children's entertainment areas, and spa services. Its beach area meets Blue Flag standards, offering safe and clean waters with sunbed service, lifeguards, and wellness activities. For direct reservations, visit www.barutlara.com/en.

Limak Lara Deluxe Hotel & Resort

Limak Lara Deluxe stands at Kemeragzi Mevkii P.K. 34, Lara, Antalya, a short drive from the international airport and directly by the coast. Rooms begin at around $305 per night under their all-inclusive model, which covers meals, drinks, and access to entertainment and recreational areas. The property includes multiple themed restaurants, pools for all ages, a full-service spa, and daily event programming for families and couples. The beach is wide and well-equipped, with water sports and shaded loungers for those spending the day by the shore. Bookings and further information are available at www.limakhotels.com/lara.

2.5 Unique Stays: Historic Buildings and Boutique Hotels

Antalya's Kaleiçi district preserves more than just the remnants of past empires—it breathes them into life through its historic lodging spaces. These boutique accommodations are not merely places to sleep but storied buildings that reflect the evolution of Anatolian culture and Ottoman design. Travelers staying in these properties engage directly with Antalya's layered past, from Roman foundations to Ottoman woodwork, without sacrificing modern conveniences.

Tuvana Hotel

Tuvana Hotel sits within Antalya's old town on Karanlık Street and has transformed an 18th-century Ottoman home into a refined boutique space. Located at Tuzcular Mahallesi, Karanlık Sokak No:18, Antalya 07100, guests can book rooms from around €99 directly at www.tuvanahotel.com. Visitors enjoy curated comforts like complimentary fruit platters and sparkling wine, with amenities that include marble bathrooms, air conditioning, and satellite TV. The hotel offers an on-site gourmet restaurant, a shaded garden courtyard, and arranged tours into the heart of Antalya's historical surroundings. Its design carefully integrates antique Turkish furnishings and wooden ceilings, preserving the texture and character of the original Ottoman residence.

Alp Paşa Hotel

Within the heart of Kaleiçi, Alp Paşa Hotel combines several old stone mansions into a boutique retreat that exudes historical elegance. Set on Hesapçı Street in the Barbaros neighbourhood, Antalya 07100, it offers stays from €90 per night via its official platform www.alppasa.com. The interiors reflect Turkish craftsmanship with tilework, carved wood accents, and restored archways blended with modern en-suite luxuries. The property boasts a swimming pool, spa services, and a restaurant built beneath old vaulted ceilings, serving dishes inspired by Ottoman cuisine. Courtyards filled with olive trees and carved fountains enhance the old-world charm, making the hotel more than just a place to rest.

Tekeli Konakları

Tekeli Konakları stands in Kaleiçi, just a short walk from Antalya's Roman Harbour, made up of carefully renovated heritage homes. It sits at Dizdar Hasan Sokak, Antalya 07100, where rooms start at €81 and are available through www.tekeli.com.tr. Guests enjoy access to a tranquil courtyard pool, breakfast service, and proximity to both the beach and key ancient landmarks. What sets this property apart is its dedication to retaining its architectural roots while providing an escape from the bustle of the modern city.

Eski Masal Hotel

Eski Masal Hotel offers an adults-only environment designed within a historical townhouse, blending Turkish stonework with understated luxury. Its location is Mescit Street No:25/1 in Muratpaşa, Antalya 07100, and suite bookings begin from around $183 at www.eskimasalhotel.com. The hotel provides individually themed suites, spa baths, fireplace lounges, and a Roman-style outdoor pool that sits quietly in its courtyard. Services include tailored breakfast options, 24-hour assistance, and private transfers, all managed by attentive staff that elevate the experience. Original walls, traditional fabrics, and curated décor give the hotel a sense of authenticity while catering to refined comfort seekers.

Patio Hotel

Tucked into the streets of Kaleiçi's old quarter, Patio Hotel occupies a restored wooden-framed Ottoman building rich in period details. It is located at Hesapçı Geçidi Street No:5, Antalya 07000, and offers budget-friendly stays from around $45, often found via www.booking.com. Rooms feature hardwood floors, air conditioning, Wi-Fi, and private bathrooms, while common areas include a shaded terrace and bar. The small size of the property ensures a more personal guest experience, enhanced by its proximity to Antalya's key historical sites. Patio Hotel appeals to visitors looking for simple charm and heritage atmosphere without sacrificing accessibility or affordability.

Hadrianus Pansion

Hadrianus Pansion offers a homely stay inside a converted Ottoman house situated on Zeytin Street, just minutes from Hadrian's Gate. Found at Kılıçaslan Mahallesi, Zeytin Sokak No:4 A/B, Antalya 07100, rooms start around $51 with bookings available through www.booked.net. Its layout includes a small garden, traditional balconies, and rooms equipped with private bathrooms, satellite TV, and climate control. The pension operates with a family-run ethos, providing breakfast service and local advice in a peaceful setting close to historical attractions. Its setting in a quiet alleyway within Kaleiçi makes it a convenient retreat for guests wanting easy access to both old town charm and the beach.

CHAPTER 3
TRANSPORTATION

3.1 Getting to Antalya

For anyone planning a journey to Antalya, the first step is understanding the most efficient and comfortable ways to arrive in this coastal Turkish city. Located on the southwestern edge of the Anatolian peninsula, Antalya is framed by the Taurus Mountains and the Mediterranean Sea, making it not just scenic but also strategically accessible. The city's rising popularity as both a tourist and business hub has significantly improved its connections with major domestic and international destinations. Travellers will find that Antalya's transit options are not only varied but also cost-effective and reliable.

Arriving in Antalya by Air

The fastest and most convenient way into Antalya is by air, with Antalya Airport (AYT) serving as the main international gateway. This modern airport is about 13 kilometres northeast of the city centre and handles both seasonal and year-round flights from across Europe, the Middle East, and within Turkey. Major international carriers such as Turkish Airlines, SunExpress, Lufthansa, Pegasus Airlines, and British Airways operate routes to Antalya, particularly in the high tourist seasons. Flights from London or Frankfurt can cost between €150 and €300 for a round trip depending on the time of booking and the season. Tickets are best booked directly through airline websites like www.turkishairlines.com, www.flypgs.com for Pegasus, or comparison portals such as www.skyscanner.com and www.kayak.com. During the summer months, charter airlines also provide direct flights from cities like Amsterdam, Moscow, and Stockholm.

From the Airport to the City Centre

Once a traveller arrives at Antalya Airport, getting into the heart of the city is straightforward and relatively inexpensive. The most convenient option is the taxi, which costs approximately 300 to 400 Turkish Lira, depending on traffic and destination. Alternatively, the HAVAŞ airport shuttle buses and tramway services connect the terminals with key parts of the city such as the central bus station, Kaleiçi, and Lara. The tram ride takes about 40 minutes and is one of the cheapest modes of transit, costing less than 20 TL with the AntalyaKart system. Car rentals are also available at the airport for those planning to explore the broader Antalya region, with reputable providers like Avis, Hertz, and Enterprise offering competitive daily rates.

Reaching Antalya by Train and Bus

While Antalya itself is not directly connected to Turkey's railway network, travellers can still incorporate rail travel into their journey. The nearest major railway station is in Burdur or Isparta, from where buses run frequently to Antalya, taking approximately two hours. More commonly, long-distance buses are used to reach Antalya from other Turkish cities. The intercity bus network in Turkey is extensive, with companies like Kamil Koç, Metro Turizm, and Pamukkale Turizm offering comfortable coach services from Istanbul, Ankara, Izmir, and other urban centres. Tickets can be booked online via each operator's official website or aggregators such as www.obilet.com or www.biletall.com.

Travelling to Antalya by Road

For visitors already in Turkey or neighbouring countries, driving to Antalya is a feasible and scenic alternative. The D400 coastal highway is particularly popular, offering dramatic views of the sea and mountains as it snakes down from Fethiye and Mersin. From Istanbul, the drive covers about 700 kilometres and takes roughly ten hours without stops, although most prefer to break the trip into parts to enjoy the diverse landscape. Roads leading into Antalya are well-maintained, and fuel stations, rest stops, and food outlets are plentiful along the way. Foreign visitors can rent vehicles in major cities and drive into Antalya with an international driver's license, keeping in mind Turkish traffic regulations and toll road charges.

Practical Tips for Booking and Planning

When planning a trip to Antalya, it pays to compare transport options well in advance, especially during the peak summer months of June through September. Booking flights at least eight weeks ahead can help secure better prices, while bus and train-linked travel require less lead time but benefit from early reservations during national holidays. It's also advisable to carry some Turkish Lira in cash, particularly for local transport and roadside services where card payment may not be accepted. Visitors should check visa requirements through www.evisa.gov.tr and ensure that all travel documents, including international driving permits if needed, are in order before departure. Whether flying in or arriving by land, the journey to Antalya can be just as enriching as the destination itself.

3.2 Public Transportation Options (Bus, Tram)

Antalya offers an efficient public transport system that simplifies movement for both locals and visitors. Travelling through Antalya becomes more immersive when one uses its buses and trams, allowing a slower, more engaged experience of its urban life. With affordable fares and regular services, it offers a practical and budget-conscious way to explore Antalya's diverse landscape.

Antalya Otobüs (City Bus Service)

The mainstay of public transportation in Antalya is its extensive city bus service, operated primarily by the Antalya Metropolitan Municipality under the name "Antalya Otobüs." These buses serve most districts including Muratpaşa, Kepez, and Konyaaltı, ensuring that every corner of the city is within reach. Visitors can ride the bus by purchasing an AntalyaKart, a contactless smart card available at kiosks, vending machines and online, which costs around ₺15 to acquire and about ₺15 per ride as of mid-2025. The buses run on fixed schedules, typically from early morning until midnight, and routes are clearly marked with LED displays. For tourists, the 600-line bus is particularly useful as it connects the city centre directly with Antalya Airport, running every 30 minutes.

Antray (Light Rail System)

This system is especially efficient for avoiding road traffic and offers a smooth ride, ideal for those commuting from the outskirts into the heart of Antalya. The trams accept the AntalyaKart and cost the same as buses, approximately ₺15 per journey. Tram stops are marked clearly and often located near key attractions, including the city museum and shopping malls. Most trams run every 10 to 15 minutes during peak hours, and they're air-conditioned, making them a preferred option during the scorching summer months.

Nostalji Tramvay (Nostalgic Tram)
Originally built in 1999, it follows a route from Zerdalilik to the Antalya Museum via Kaleiçi and Cumhuriyet Square, tracing a line that covers both cultural and commercial landmarks. It is slower and shorter in route than Antray, but it offers an old-world experience that fits perfectly with the charm of Antalya's historic core. Fares remain standard and can be paid using the AntalyaKart, and its carriages are designed in classic European style. This tram is particularly popular with tourists who wish to take photographs and absorb the character of the old city while in transit.

Dolmuş (Shared Minibus Service)
Though not operated by the municipal authority, the dolmuş services in Antalya form an informal yet vital component of public transport, especially for routes not covered by standard buses. These shared minibuses operate on semi-fixed routes and can be flagged down from almost anywhere along their path, offering flexibility. Fares are usually cash-based and cost between ₺10 and ₺20 depending on distance, and they are paid directly to the driver. Dolmuş vehicles connect suburbs, coastal areas, and even outlying towns, offering a grassroots glimpse into local life. For many, this is the most authentic form of travel, full of spontaneity and interaction.

AntalyaKart (Smart Ticketing System)
The backbone of fare payment for all official public transportation in Antalya is the AntalyaKart, which simplifies access to buses, trams, and even certain municipal facilities. The card can be purchased at vending machines located in major terminals or recharging points throughout the city. Tourists can also buy temporary or disposable cards if they plan a short stay. Topping up is straightforward and can be done using cash or credit card, and balances can be monitored online or via the mobile app. The convenience of the AntalyaKart lies in its integration—users need only one card for the whole system, and transfers between bus and tram are discounted if made within a time window.

Airport Bus (Line 600 and 800)

For new arrivals, the airport bus lines—specifically Line 600 (to Antalya Bus Terminal) and Line 800 (to Lara)—are a dependable way to reach the city without resorting to taxis. These buses operate regularly, with services every 30 to 60 minutes, and cover major city points, including public squares, hotels, and shopping centres. The fare is covered by the AntalyaKart and typically falls under ₺15, making it a far more economical option compared to private transfers. The vehicles are clean, equipped with luggage space, and operate between 6 a.m. and midnight, though schedules may vary seasonally. It's a solid option for visitors arriving late or travelling on a tighter budget.

3.3 Taxi Services

Taxis in Antalya offer visitors a blend of convenience and local insight, whisking them from sun-drenched beaches to ancient ruins with ease. The citywide network operates around the clock, ensuring that whether arriving on a red-eye flight or exploring twilight bazaars, transport remains at hand. Metered fares adhere to municipal regulations, yet drivers often welcome brief chats about hidden gems off the beaten path.

Antalya Taksi

Antalya Taksi stands as the city's cornerstone taxi provider, easily recognizable by its yellow and white vehicles. The official meter begins at 6.00 Turkish lira and advances approximately 3.70 lira per kilometer during daylight hours. Two surcharge tiers apply: a fifty-percent premium for airport pickups and a twenty-percent increase between midnight and dawn. Management can be reached by dialing +90 242 334 44 44 or via the Antalya Taksi mobile app, available for Android and iOS. Stands cluster around major transport hubs including the airport, Otogar central bus station, and Atatürk Park.

Lara Taksi

Lara Taksi caters predominantly to the eastern suburbs and beachfront resorts stretching toward Kemer. Metres start at 6.50 lira, reflecting slightly longer initial distances from residential enclaves to the seaside boulevard. Passengers can request a vehicle through the Lara Taksi hotline at +90 242 323 21 21 or flag one down at designated stands near large hotels. Night journeys incur a twenty-percent fee, while luggage assistance typically adds an extra 5 lira to the final bill. Drivers often add personalized suggestions for Marmara beach bars and off-peak swim spots in the Kiriş district.

Konyaaltı Taksi

Konyaaltı Taksi dominates the western shoreline, ferrying passengers along the palm-lined promenade between Konyaaltı Beach and the city centre. Visitors should expect a 6.00 lira start fee and roughly 3.70 lira per kilometer, consistent with municipal tariffs. Hailing is simple via the Konyaaltı Taksi mobile application or by visiting harbour-adjacent stands near the Akdeniz University campus. When traveling with pets or surfboards, a modest 5 lira surcharge covers additional cleaning and space requirements. The fleet includes wheelchair-accessible vehicles, bookable in advance by phone to ensure barrier-free transfers.

Düden Taksi

Düden Taksi services the northern quarters around the Düden Waterfalls and suburban districts of Kepez. Standard fares align with citywide rates: a 6.00 lira pickup charge and circa 3.70 lira per kilometer after. According to customer reviews, drivers are well acquainted with scenic routes, elevating the journey with historic anecdotes. Hotline reservations at +90 242 266 66 66 guarantee vehicle dispatch within ten minutes during peak hours. For expeditions to the Cascading Düden, negotiate flat-rate day tours for convenience and local expertise.

Kepez Taksi

Kepez Taksi operates deeper inland, delivering seamless connections between residential zones and Antalya's vibrant centre. Messaging requests via WhatsApp to +90 242 221 11 11 often yield quicker confirmations than traditional calls. The initial 6.00 lira fare applies, with variable per-kilometer fees that reflect the city's traffic conditions at different times of day. Drivers are accustomed to multi-stop itineraries, though guests should clarify stops beforehand to avoid unexpected charges. Strategically placed stands at street corners near Kepez Municipality buildings host ready taxis throughout daylight hours.

3.4 Car Rentals and Driving Tips

Exploring Antalya by car offers visitors an unmatched level of freedom to discover the beauty of Turkey's Mediterranean coast, from its rugged inland mountains to hidden coves and ancient ruins. While public transport serves the basics, a rental car provides access to places untouched by bus routes and tight schedules. In Turkey, driving is on the right, and most road signs are in both

Turkish and English, which eases navigation. Highways are generally well maintained, though rural routes can be narrow and winding.

Circular Car Hire

Circular Car Hire operates directly at Antalya Airport, located near the arrivals gate on Cumhuriyet Caddesi No:82, Aksu. They're open around the clock and offer a smooth meet-and-greet service for all incoming flights. The company caters to various budgets, with daily prices starting around $54.40 for compact vehicles, scaling up with more luxurious models. Booking is handled through their local website, which supports English, and any questions can be directed to their responsive local numbers: +90 532 783 9531 and +90 536 283 2415. They offer unlimited mileage and a full-to-full fuel policy, with flexible pick-up and drop-off locations across the Antalya region, making them a practical choice for travelers on diverse itineraries.

Ace Rent A Car

Ace Rent A Car serves both domestic and international travelers from its desk inside the domestic terminal of Antalya Airport. Their location at Yesilkoy Mahallesi ensures convenience for arrivals from other Turkish cities. Bookings can be made via their global website, with rates beginning from €35 per day for small cars and rising based on model and season. Customer inquiries are handled locally through +90 507 121 6284. All vehicles include insurance and are serviced to international standards, with options for manual and automatic transmission. Fuel terms are full-to-full, and a courtesy shuttle is available to selected hotels within the Antalya city limits.

Europcar

Europcar maintains several branches in Antalya, including a prominent outlet in the airport terminal and another downtown office at Zemin Kat No 183a, Muratpaşa. The company offers an extensive vehicle selection, with rates for economy cars starting at roughly $39 daily. Their international booking system allows users to earn loyalty points and choose from multiple insurance packages. For assistance, local representatives are available via the website or directly at the branch. Vehicles come with unlimited mileage and roadside assistance, and the fuel policy follows the industry standard of full-to-full.

Avis

Avis has an accessible location in Antalya's Domestic Terminal, where staff greet customers at the luggage area and escort them to the car pick-up point. Online reservations through their official site show base prices from $31 per day, with discounts for weekly rentals pushing full-week rates to around $250 for standard sedans. Contact can be made through local branches or international hotlines, and vehicles are typically issued with a full tank of fuel. Avis also provides GPS navigation, additional driver options, and baby seats for families. After-hours returns are handled by a secure key-drop system near the terminal parking lot.

Hertz

Hertz operates from two locations within Antalya Airport, including an outlet inside Terminal 1, making pick-up fast and efficient no matter which airline you fly. Their pricing begins at approximately $38 per day for basic models, with tiered rates depending on the size and class of the vehicle. Hertz provides third-party liability and collision damage waivers as part of their rental packages. Additional perks like the Hertz Gold Plus program allow for queue-free pick-ups, and fuel arrangements are customizable at the time of booking.

Garenta

Garenta, a local Turkish brand, offers rentals at highly competitive prices from their office within the domestic arrivals section at Antalya Airport, located in the Muratpaşa district. Starting rates can be as low as €13.83 for a mini car, increasing with vehicle class and specifications. Reservations can be managed online at garenta.com.tr or by contacting their central call service at 444 5 478. Garenta's fleet features both manual and automatic transmissions, and drivers must be at least 21 years old with a license held for over 12 months. Cars are supplied with full tanks, and the company provides extras such as winter tyres and toll devices upon request.

3.5 Airport Transfers and Shuttle Services

Antalya International Airport welcomes millions of passengers every year, many of whom head directly to the vibrant city of Antalya or its surrounding beach resorts. Efficient airport transfers are vital here, especially considering the distance between the terminals and city centre. With a wide range of services on offer, from budget-friendly group shuttles to luxury private vehicles, visitors can

35

choose what suits their budget and travel style. Most services operate with fixed rates, round-the-clock availability, and the added convenience of advance booking.

Havaş Airport Shuttle
The Havaş shuttle remains a popular option for those heading into Antalya city from the airport, especially among local travellers. The service departs hourly, starting from early morning until late at night, and has a night run scheduled around 1:30 a.m. Boarding points are clearly marked outside the domestic terminal, and international travellers can follow signs to the domestic pickup area. A typical journey into town takes around 35 minutes and costs 160 Turkish Lira per person. Passengers can pay at the shuttle desk or directly to the driver, with mobile bookings available for added convenience.

Shuttle Board Antalya
Shuttle Board operates shared minibus services catering to those seeking low-cost transportation from the airport to central Antalya. With departures scheduled every two hours during daytime, the service is suitable for solo tourists and small groups alike. On arrival, passengers can locate the Shuttle Board kiosk near the terminal exit, where staff confirm bookings and provide directions. Each ride is priced at €3 per passenger, and the route generally includes hotels and neighbourhoods within the main city limits. Reservations can be made online to secure a seat in advance, especially during high season.

Side Shuttle Transfers
This provider focuses on destinations outside central Antalya, especially the tourist-favoured region of Side and nearby resort zones such as Kumköy and Evrenseki. Travellers booking in advance are met at the arrivals gate by drivers holding name cards, ensuring quick and smooth handovers. Each transfer to Side or its adjacent areas is priced at USD 22 per person. Vehicles depart shortly after peak flight arrivals, and payment is accepted either during booking or directly in cash. For visitors heading to the beach resorts east of Antalya, this service is both reliable and cost-effective.

Hoppa Transfers
Hoppa operates as an online aggregator, offering customers the ability to choose between private cars, minibuses and shared coaches at competitive prices. Starting at around £9.15 per passenger, the platform allows users to pre-book

their journey with the assurance of fixed pricing and instant confirmation. Hoppa's drivers monitor incoming flights to adjust pickup times accordingly, and passengers are met in the arrivals area for a direct and timely transfer. The service covers destinations throughout Antalya and its outskirts, with a reputation for reliability and responsive customer support.

AirportTransfer724 Antalya

This company is geared towards those seeking personalised, private transport from Antalya Airport to various locations across the region. A ride into central Antalya typically costs €26, while trips to further resorts such as Belek or Alanya are priced between €39 and €46 depending on distance. Passengers are greeted at the terminal with a name placard, and the fare includes all tolls and parking fees. Bookings must be made in advance via their website, and full payment is processed securely by card with no additional charges at drop-off. Their service also tracks delays automatically to ensure timely pick-up.

İyiTransfer Executive Service

İyiTransfer stands out by offering upscale transport options tailored to groups, families, and VIP clients. Travellers can book a high-end Mercedes Vito for up to six passengers at a cost of 1,400 Turkish Lira, or opt for a larger Sprinter minibus accommodating up to thirteen people for around 1,600 Turkish Lira. Reservations can be made directly on their site or by messaging them on WhatsApp. Drivers wait just outside the arrivals area and provide luggage assistance. Services are flexible, offering free cancellation up to a day before, with custom options for guests needing accessible or child-friendly transport.

CHAPTER 4
TOP ATTRACTIONS & HIDDEN GEMS

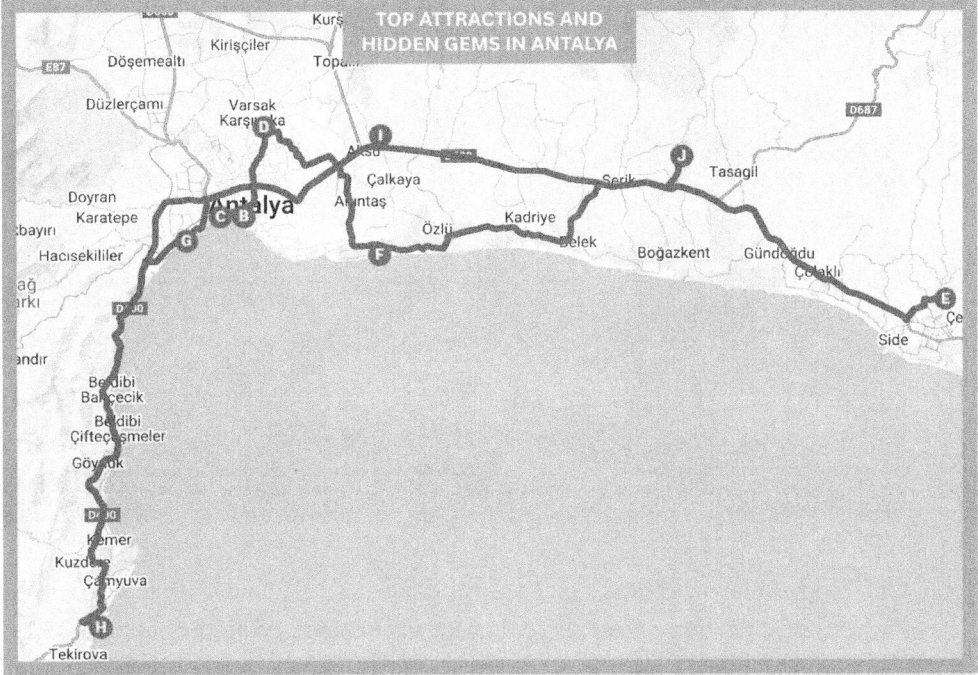

Directions from Selçuk, Kaleiçi, Muratpaşa/Antalya, Türkiye to Aspendos Theatre, Belkıs, Aspendos Yolu, Serik/Antalya, Türkiye

A
Selçuk, Kaleiçi,
Muratpaşa/Antalya, Türkiye

F
Lara Beach,
Antalya, Türkiye

B
Yivliminare Mosque, Selçuk, Korkut Sokak,
Muratpaşa/Antalya, Türkiye

G
Konyaaltı Beaches, Meltem,
Muratpaşa/Antalya, Türkiye

C
Antalya Museum, Bahçelievler, Konyaaltı
Caddesi, Muratpaşa/Antalya, Türkiye

H
Phaselis Ancient City,
Tekirova, Kemer/Antalya, Türkiye

D
Duden Waterfalls, Habibler,
Kepez/Antalya, Türkiye

I
Perge Ancient City, Barbaros,
Perge Yolu, Aksu/Antalya, Türkiye

E
Flow Manavgat Waterfall, Sarılar, istiklal
caddesi, Manavgat/Antalya, Türkiye

J
Aspendos Theatre, Belkıs,
Aspendos Yolu, Serik/Antalya, Türkiye

4.1 Old Town (Kaleiçi)

Old Town Antalya, known locally as Kaleiçi, is more than a historic district; it is the soul of the city, a place where time seems to pause. Winding cobbled streets, Ottoman-era houses with ornate bay windows, Roman relics, and Byzantine remnants create a tapestry of heritage that pulls visitors into centuries of cultural exchange. Surrounded by ancient walls and opening onto the glistening blue waters of the Mediterranean, Kaleiçi is a must-visit enclave that tells Antalya's story through its architecture, monuments, and atmosphere.

Hadrian's Gate

Located at the eastern entrance of Kaleiçi, it is easily accessible on foot from any part of the Old Town and serves as a dramatic entry point into history. With no entry fee, visitors are free to walk under its marble arches, flanked by ancient towers, and admire the detailed Corinthian columns and inscriptions. Its three barrel-vaulted arches and preserved stonework give a direct view into Roman engineering and imperial symbolism. The gate is especially magical at dusk, when lighting enhances its carvings and transports you to the grandeur of ancient Pamphylia.

Yivli Minaret Mosque (Ulu Cami)

The Yivli Minaret Mosque is an architectural and religious icon, with its fluted minaret rising unmistakably above Antalya's skyline. Located near the city's central Cumhuriyet Square, this 13th-century Seljuk masterpiece is accessible by a short walk from anywhere within Kaleiçi. Entry is free, and respectful attire is expected inside, as it remains an active place of worship. The mosque is part of a larger complex that includes madrasas and tombs, offering insight into the spiritual and academic life of medieval Anatolia. Visitors can admire the intricate brickwork of the minaret, explore the peaceful courtyard, and absorb the quiet reverence that still pervades this ancient sanctuary.

Hıdırlık Tower
The Hıdırlık Tower watches over the edge of Kaleiçi where the old city walls meet the sea, its cylindrical structure looming above Karaalioğlu Park and the harbour below. Built by the Romans in the 2nd century and later modified by Seljuks and Ottomans, the tower has served as both a fortification and lighthouse. It's free to view from the outside, and though the interior isn't open for entry, the panoramic views from the base—especially at sunset—are breathtaking. It's a five-minute walk from Hadrian's Gate or the marina, making it a popular detour on a walking tour. The site is a favourite for photography and contemplation, offering both natural beauty and historical gravity.

Antalya Ethnographic Museum (Suna-Inan Kıraç Kaleiçi Museum)
Nestled in a restored 19th-century mansion near Mermerli Street, the Antalya Ethnographic Museum provides a vivid look into Ottoman life through furnished rooms, costumes, and everyday artefacts. It's a short stroll from the main Kaleiçi harbour area and charges a modest entry fee, typically around 2 to 3 euros. The museum complex includes a Greek Orthodox church converted into an exhibition space, showcasing cultural coexistence in Anatolia's past. Visitors can wander through courtyards and study traditional Turkish living arrangements, gaining deep insights into gender roles, family life, and domestic architecture. It is a rare chance to step beyond the stones of antiquity and into the rhythms of ordinary lives once lived here.

Antalya Marina and Harbour
The Old Harbour of Antalya, tucked below Kaleiçi's cliffs, is where history and leisure blend seamlessly, offering a stunning view of turquoise waters framed by ancient stone walls. Easily reached by descending the stone path from the central square or taking the glass elevator, the marina is free to access and always buzzing with energy. Once a key Mediterranean trade hub, it now welcomes yachts, tour boats, and local fishing vessels, creating a picturesque

waterfront. Visitors can dine at cliffside cafes, take boat tours along the coast, or simply relax to the sound of waves and gulls. It's the perfect place to conclude a day exploring Kaleiçi—calm, charming, and utterly unforgettable.

4.2 Yivliminare Mosque

The Yivliminare Mosque, known as the "Fluted Minaret Mosque," is not just one of Antalya's most iconic landmarks—it is a cradle of Anatolian Seljuk heritage and a beacon of Islamic architecture. Located in the heart of Kaleiçi, this 13th-century mosque is distinguished by its fluted brick minaret rising to 38 metres, a structure that has come to symbolise the city itself. Yet beyond its recognisable exterior lies a complex that once functioned as a külliye—a communal religious compound—housing various significant buildings each with a unique historical narrative.

Yivliminare Mosque Prayer Hall

The mosque's design showcases early Anatolian Seljuk architecture with six domes supported by stone piers and arches, creating a spacious and austere interior. Entry is free, but modest dress is required as it is still an active house of worship. It is located just off Cumhuriyet Square and is easily reached on foot from any part of Kaleiçi. Standing inside, one can feel the quiet rhythm of time and admire the blend of simplicity and grandeur that characterises early Turkish mosques.

Yivliminare Minaret

The fluted minaret itself is one of the oldest surviving examples of Islamic architecture in the region, built in 1230 under the Seljuk Sultan Alaaddin Keykubat I. Though not accessible from the inside, its exterior is best admired from multiple angles throughout the courtyard and surrounding alleys. The turquoise glazed tiles that once adorned it still cling to parts of the surface, hinting at its original splendour. Towering above Kaleiçi, the minaret acts as both a landmark and a cultural signpost, drawing travellers in to explore what lies beneath. It's especially impressive at twilight, when the structure glows under floodlights and casts long shadows over the mosque complex.

Gıyaseddin Keyhüsrev Madrasah Ruins

Adjacent to the mosque are the weathered remains of a Seljuk-era madrasah, once a centre of theological and scientific education during the 13th century. While only traces of the original building remain, they reveal the layout of an institution that trained scholars, judges, and religious leaders for generations. Visitors can walk through the courtyard where students once debated Islamic law, astronomy, and philosophy. Entry is free, and it's located just steps from the mosque's prayer hall, making it an easy inclusion in any visit. These ruins, though modest, offer a powerful glimpse into the intellectual life that flourished under Seljuk rule.

Tombs of Zincirkıran Mehmet Bey and Nigar Hatun

Within the Yivliminare Mosque complex lie two historically significant tombs—those of Zincirkıran Mehmet Bey, an Ottoman admiral, and Nigar Hatun, the wife of Sultan Bayezid II. Both tombs are simple yet evocative, built in traditional Ottoman style with domed roofs and stone grave markers. Located in a quiet corner of the complex and open without charge, they provide visitors a moment of reflection on the lives of two influential figures from Ottoman history. These tombs are not only places of rest but also of remembrance, echoing the legacy of an empire that shaped Antalya's destiny. Visiting them lends a personal human layer to the architectural and religious experience of the mosque.

Mevlevihane Lodge (Dervish Lodge)

Housed within a repurposed section of the mosque complex, the Mevlevihane Lodge once hosted followers of the Mevlevi Order—better known as the Whirling Dervishes. Today it serves as an exhibition hall or museum, though in earlier centuries it was a spiritual retreat where rituals, music, and prayer merged into transcendental experience. The lodge reflects Sufi philosophy through its design and peaceful ambiance, inviting visitors to consider a softer, mystical dimension of Islam. Easily accessible from the mosque's western side, its small garden and stone hall are often missed by hurried tourists. Those who linger here are rewarded with quiet insight into a deeply poetic tradition of Turkish spirituality.

4.3 Antalya Museum

Situated in the Konyaaltı district, just west of Antalya's city centre, the museum houses an astonishing collection of artifacts that chronicle the depth and breadth of Anatolian history. Accessible by tram from Kaleiçi or local buses, it invites travellers to step beyond modern Antalya and into the lives of ancient civilizations. The museum charges a modest entrance fee—usually around 200 Turkish Lira—and remains open most days except Mondays.

The Hall of Gods

This gallery is a treasure trove of classical mythology, showcasing statues of ancient deities excavated from Perge, Side, and other Pamphylian cities. Standing tall and majestic are the marble figures of Zeus, Athena, Artemis, Hermes, and Apollo—each masterfully sculpted and steeped in millennia of worship. The arrangement allows visitors to almost breathe the air of ancient sanctuaries, immersing themselves in what once was divine to ancient cultures. Beyond the artistic allure, this hall tells a story of belief, power, and the fusion of Greek and Roman identities in Anatolia. The atmosphere here is reverent and majestic, evoking awe with every quiet step across the polished floor.

The Mosaic Hall

The intricately preserved mosaics in this section are a mosaic of history in themselves, originating from Roman villas and bathhouses that once graced Antalya's coastal cities. These vivid floor masterpieces capture scenes of mythology, marine life, and daily existence with a level of craftsmanship that echoes across centuries. Displayed with careful lighting and restored fragments, the room speaks to both the decadence and sophistication of Roman domestic life. This hall isn't just about art, it's about storytelling through stone and pigment, silent but eloquent. A visitor will find themselves lingering, piecing together the everyday lives of people who lived, laughed, and loved over 1,500 years ago.

The Hall of Emperors

This section houses monumental statues and busts of Roman emperors, from Hadrian to Septimius Severus, originally discovered in Perge and Sagalassos. Each sculpture is a triumph of imperial propaganda, chiseled to convey strength, dignity, and divinity through the ages. Visitors walking through these marble faces of power can almost feel the politics and prestige of Rome at its eastern frontier. The historical resonance here is unmistakable—this isn't mere display, it's a confrontation with history's most commanding personalities. As light pours in subtly from the ceiling, the atmosphere lends itself to quiet contemplation and powerful reflection.

The Sarcophagus Hall

Towering sarcophagi, intricately carved with scenes from mythology and ancient life, dominate this sombre yet grand gallery. Chief among them is the Heracles Sarcophagus, a stunning piece discovered in Perge and repatriated from abroad after a long legal battle. These massive stone coffins are more than tombs—they're chapters of cultural pride, religious symbolism, and funerary artistry. As you walk among them, the stillness is broken only by the whisper of history that speaks from each relief and inscription. The room conveys an eerie beauty, where death and legacy are woven seamlessly into artistic grandeur.

Children's Section and Prehistoric Hall

Dedicated to engaging younger minds, this area is an interactive blend of education and discovery, adjacent to the museum's earliest chronological exhibits. Here, simple stone tools, Neolithic figurines, and primitive ceramics are paired with child-friendly displays, creating a timeline that runs from cave life to city-states. It's a place that nurtures curiosity, making archaeology approachable for all ages and sparking the wonder that fuels lifelong learning. This hall bridges the raw simplicity of ancient existence with the joyful complexity of modern exploration. For families and solo travellers alike, it offers a refreshing change of pace in an otherwise intense historical setting.

4.4 Düden Waterfalls

Located roughly 10 kilometres northeast of Antalya's city centre, Düden Waterfalls is accessible by car, local buses, and organised tours, while Lower Düden spills dramatically off a cliff into the Mediterranean near Lara. Entry to the Upper Düden Waterfalls usually requires a small fee, while the lower section remains free to admire from parks and viewpoints.

Upper Düden Waterfalls
Upper Düden Waterfalls is nestled in the Kepez district and offers a serene, forested escape within a carefully managed nature park. Visitors are greeted by the thundering water that tumbles into a turquoise basin, surrounded by moss-covered rocks and shaded by overhanging trees. One of the highlights is the chance to walk behind the falls through a shallow cave, where the sound and spray create an exhilarating experience. There's a modest entrance fee, but the beauty of the falls, coupled with facilities like tea gardens and shaded benches, makes it entirely worthwhile. This upper section is perfect for families, couples, and photographers looking to slow down and savour the rhythm of nature.

Cave Behind the Falls
A distinctive feature of the Upper Düden site is the hidden cave path that snakes behind the waterfall, offering a completely immersive encounter with this

natural spectacle. From this position, you can see the cascading water from the inside out, with sunlight filtering through the spray in a mesmerising dance. The air here is cool and damp, and the constant roar adds a dramatic soundtrack as you pass through. It's a rare geological setup that lets visitors explore a waterfall from within, providing a perspective few places on earth can match. This shaded enclave is not just a photo opportunity—it's a moment of elemental closeness to the power of water itself.

Lower Düden Waterfalls
Lower Düden Waterfalls, also known as Karpuzkaldıran, offers a cinematic finale as the river plunges straight off the cliffs into the Mediterranean Sea. Located near Lara, this dramatic coastal scene is best viewed from Düden Park, which stretches along the cliffs and offers landscaped trails, cafes, and benches overlooking the sea. There's no entrance fee here, and the park is open all day, making it a favourite for both romantic sunsets and midday strolls. Boat tours from Kaleiçi harbour also provide a striking ocean-facing view of the falls tumbling into the sea. It is an awe-inspiring reminder of Antalya's unique blend of nature and geography.

Düden Park Cliff Walk
Düden Park, where the Lower Düden Waterfall crashes into the sea, provides more than just a viewpoint—it offers a landscaped clifftop promenade with breath-catching sea vistas. The walk takes visitors through manicured lawns, under pergolas, past sculptures, and finally to the cliff's edge where the roar of the water punctuates the horizon. Street vendors selling roasted corn and ice cream add a relaxed local flavour, while shaded seating areas invite lingering. This stretch is free to access and accessible by public buses heading toward Lara from central Antalya. It's a place where locals come to unwind and visitors discover Antalya's deeper connection between nature and urban life.

Picnic and Recreation Areas at Upper Düden
Upper Düden Waterfalls is more than just a viewing platform—it's a well-laid-out park with shaded picnic areas, kiosks, and family-friendly spots to rest and eat. Surrounded by thick greenery and the sound of running water, these areas make it ideal for long afternoon visits. You can bring your own picnic basket or enjoy light Turkish meals at the on-site cafés and food stalls, many of which serve gözleme and tea. The space is popular on weekends with both locals and travellers, and its cleanliness and upkeep ensure a comfortable stay.

4.5 Manavgat Waterfalls

The Manavgat Waterfalls represent a soul-stirring retreat from the bustle of the city. Located just 3 kilometres north of Manavgat town and about 80 kilometres east of Antalya, this serene site draws visitors seeking nature's quieter grandeur. The waterfalls are not towering, but their wide, thunderous curtain creates an immersive experience of sound and spray. With shaded tea gardens, riverside eateries, and platforms for photos, it becomes a haven for families, couples, and solo explorers alike. Entry usually costs around 10 TL, and reaching it is easy via local dolmuş or guided excursions from Side or Antalya.

Manavgat Waterfall Viewpoint and Terrace
The most photographed part of the area, the designated viewing platform, is where the thunderous sheet of water can be admired in full, framed by flowering shrubs and hanging trees. It allows visitors to stand almost at water level, close enough to feel the cooling mist that rises off the rocks. This terrace, built for panoramic views, is ideal for quiet contemplation or capturing Instagram-worthy shots with the foamy river beneath. Access to the terrace is included in the modest entrance fee, and local kiosks nearby sell fresh pomegranate juice and handmade souvenirs. It's a simple pleasure but unforgettable, especially when the morning light hits the water just right.

Manavgat River Cruise Boarding Point

Just downstream from the falls lies the Manavgat River cruise pier, where boats embark on a tranquil journey toward the sea, blending nature, leisure, and culture in one outing. These cruises often last a few hours, with stops for swimming or a traditional Turkish lunch onboard, and provide a different vantage point of the riverside ecosystem. Boarding is possible at several jetties near the falls, and ticket prices vary, usually starting from 150 TL depending on services offered. The riverbanks are rich in birdlife, and the cruise often passes by reed beds and fishing villages. It's a must for anyone wanting to see the Mediterranean landscape unfold in slow motion.

The Fish Restaurants by the Falls

Bordering the roar of the water are a cluster of small yet authentic Turkish eateries that specialise in grilled trout and freshly baked flatbreads, prepared over open wood fires. Dining here becomes an immersive cultural experience, where the aroma of spices mingles with the earthy scent of wet leaves and river breeze. The seating is typically outdoors, shaded by massive trees and cooled by the natural humidity of the falls. Prices are modest, with meals costing between 80–150 TL, and service is often as warm as the tea served in tulip-shaped glasses. It's more than just food—it's memory-making beside the rush of nature's rhythm.

The Shaded Picnic Gardens

Tucked under towering plane trees, the picnic gardens beside the Manavgat Waterfalls offer a peaceful escape where families and travellers can rest, snack or simply listen to the roar of cascading water nearby. Wooden benches, stone tables, and hammocks allow for hours of quiet reflection or social joy, with views of the river gliding past in the distance. These areas are free to use and popular with locals during weekends, giving visitors a glimpse into the slow, family-oriented pace of Turkish countryside life. Vendors pass by selling gözleme (stuffed flatbread) and sweet corn, adding rustic charm to the atmosphere.

The Artisan Market and Local Handicrafts Stalls

A small but vibrant artisan market thrives near the main entrance, where local craftspeople display handmade jewellery, ceramics, spices, and embroidered textiles unique to the Manavgat region. The market offers more than trinkets—it's a window into local culture, a chance to speak with artisans who carry on traditions passed down through generations. Prices are often negotiable, and each piece carries a story, whether it's a carved olivewood bowl or a woven scarf dyed with natural pigments. Open year-round, this market is an ideal place to support the local economy while taking home a tangible piece of Antalya's soul. Shopping here is as much about conversation as it is about commerce.

4.6 Lara Beach

Lara Beach is a sun-drenched universe of pleasure, style, and culture carved along Antalya's southern edge. Situated just 18 kilometres east of Antalya's city centre, this coastal paradise is easily accessible by local buses, rental cars, or taxis, making it a convenient retreat for both locals and tourists. Known for its golden sands, clear waters, and proximity to world-class resorts, Lara Beach blends relaxation with a hint of modern luxury. It is free to enter, although certain private sections charge for sunbeds and cabanas.

Lara Beach Public Park (Lara Halk Plajı)

This wide, well-maintained public section of the beach offers a welcoming environment for families, backpackers, and solo travellers seeking the sea without a price tag. Open to everyone, it provides clean changing facilities, picnic spots under tamarisk trees, and free access to the coastline's gentle surf. It is especially popular in the late afternoons when locals gather with their samovars and snacks, watching the sun dip behind the Taurus Mountains. Getting here from Antalya is simple using the LC07 or KL08 buses, which stop right by the entrance. This spot reflects the egalitarian soul of Turkish coastal life—sun, sea, and a sense of belonging for all.

Sandland Antalya (Antalya Kum Heykel Müzesi)

One of the more unusual yet enchanting attractions near Lara Beach is Sandland, an open-air museum of giant sand sculptures crafted by artists from around the world. Located just off the main Lara coastal road, this temporary wonderland is rebuilt annually with themes ranging from mythology to world landmarks, drawing families and art lovers alike. Entry costs around 250 TL for adults, and the magic is best seen in the evening when sculptures are illuminated, creating a dreamlike atmosphere. There's also a section where visitors can try their hand at sculpting, adding a hands-on twist to the visit.

Lower Düden Waterfalls (Karpuzkaldıran Şelalesi)

At the far western edge of Lara Beach stands one of the most dramatic sights in Antalya—the Lower Düden Waterfalls, where the river meets the sea in a roaring cascade that drops from 40 metres into the Mediterranean. Easily reachable by foot, bike, or a short taxi ride from the beach area, this natural spectacle sits within a municipal park that is free to enter and well-equipped with viewing platforms. It's a powerful contrast to the calmness of the beach, offering a refreshing dose of nature's raw energy. Nearby cafés and shaded benches make it a perfect spot for a scenic break or picnic with a dramatic backdrop. The crashing waters here echo with nature's timeless rhythm.

Lara Beach Resorts and Theme Hotels

What makes Lara Beach truly unique in Turkey is its collection of ultra-luxury, themed resorts—full-scale recreations of famous landmarks like the Kremlin, the Titanic, and Venice, turned into lavish accommodations. These resorts are not just places to sleep but entire fantasy worlds, often all-inclusive, with aqua parks, entertainment shows, and private beachfronts. Booking prices vary seasonally, starting from around 4,000 TL per night, with reservations made easily through their official websites or platforms like Booking.com. Even if not staying there, visitors can admire the architectural boldness from the outside or attend special shows and concerts held on the premises. It's an extravagant slice of escapism, tailor-made for those who dream bigger on holiday.

TerraCity Shopping Mall

Just a short drive inland from Lara Beach lies TerraCity, one of Antalya's most upscale shopping destinations, offering a break from sand and sea with air-conditioned comfort and urban indulgence. Housing global fashion brands, fine restaurants, and a modern cinema, it provides a cosmopolitan twist to a beachside holiday. Entry is free, and most visitors spend an hour or two wandering its gleaming halls, with prices that reflect both international luxury and local bargains. Regular shuttle buses run between the mall and key resort zones, making access seamless for those without cars. Whether for branded shopping or a quiet café lunch, it adds depth and diversity to Lara's charm.

4.7 Konyaaltı Beach

Stretching for over 7 kilometres, Konyaaltı Beach is not only a place to bask in the sun, but a gateway to numerous must-see attractions nestled nearby. With easy accessibility from central Antalya, either by tram, taxi, or public bus, Konyaaltı offers more than just sea and sun; it presents a rich medley of experiences that make any visit to Antalya incomplete without stepping foot here.

Antalya Aquarium

Located just a short stroll from the main promenade of Konyaaltı Beach, Antalya Aquarium is one of the largest of its kind in the world and a crown jewel for family-friendly entertainment. Home to a 131-metre-long tunnel tank and over 40 thematic aquariums, it offers a surreal dive into marine life from around the globe. Accessible by bus from city centre or by foot from beachside hotels, entry costs around 490 TL for adults and slightly less for children. The Snow World and Ice Museum within its complex adds a contrasting wintry twist in the middle of the Mediterranean. Its imaginative blend of education, technology, and fun makes it a perfect spot for both children and adults seeking to enrich their beachside experience.

Aqualand Antalya Dolphinland

This long-standing water park and dolphin show arena allows visitors to interact with marine mammals or simply relax amidst thrilling water slides and splash pools. Easily reachable via Konyaaltı tram or local dolmuş minibus, it charges a modest entrance fee depending on the season and the activities selected. Children especially delight in the performances by dolphins and sea lions, which are run under humane and supervised conditions. The park is an ideal break from beach lounging and a thrilling alternative during the hot afternoon hours.

Atatürk Culture Park and Glass Pyramid

Lying just inland from the beach's eastern end, the Atatürk Culture Park offers a peaceful, shaded retreat filled with winding paths, manicured gardens, and an artistic soul. At its centre stands the striking Glass Pyramid (Cam Piramit), an architectural marvel that hosts concerts, exhibitions, and festivals throughout the year. A short walk from the beach or a brief tram ride drops visitors near its gates, and entry is often free unless there's a special event. Its tranquil green spaces provide a contrasting counterpoint to the lively beachfront, offering a place for reflection, art appreciation, or simply a scenic picnic. The complex pays homage to modern Turkish cultural identity while keeping its arms wide open to international expressions.

Beach Park Antalya

Right along the coastline, adjacent to the main sandy belt of Konyaaltı, lies Beach Park—a sprawling open space filled with beach clubs, eateries, cafes, and recreational zones. Open to the public and free to access, this area is where Antalya's youthful energy buzzes most visibly, particularly during evenings when live music, hookah lounges, and outdoor cinemas spring to life. Just steps away from the waves and easily reachable on foot or by bike, it's the perfect place to drift from sunbathing into sunset cocktails. The park blends seaside relaxation with urban leisure, giving every traveller a chance to experience Antalya's social life firsthand. The atmosphere is vibrant, yet still comfortably laid-back for solo travellers, families, and couples alike.

Tunektepe Cable Car (Tünektepe Teleferik)

The base station is located just a 10-minute drive or short bus ride from Konyaaltı Beach, and the round-trip fare is around 100 TL. At the top, visitors find a scenic café and observation deck perfect for photography or simply taking in the sunset over the sea. Historically used as a lookout, the hilltop retains a sense of commanding tranquility that contrasts beautifully with the bustle of the shoreline. It's a must for those who crave both thrill and serenity in one sweeping experience.

4.8 Phaselis Ancient City

Phaselis Ancient City is one of Antalya's most captivating heritage treasures. Located near Tekirova and around 60 kilometres southwest of Antalya city, this ancient Lycian harbour settlement once thrived as a maritime and commercial powerhouse. Today, it stands quietly within a national park, inviting travellers to walk among ruins that whisper of Roman emperors, Byzantine traders, and Lycian ingenuity. The entry fee is approximately 90 TL, and the site can be reached by car, taxi or via day tours from Antalya or Kemer.

The Ancient Harbour Streets

At the heart of Phaselis lies its famed central street, stretching between the city's two harbours and flanked by towering stone columns and fallen lintels. This 24-metre-wide Roman avenue, still proudly intact in many places, once echoed with merchant footsteps and ceremonial processions. Visitors walking its length today will pass by ruined shops, fountains, and carved stonework, immersed in a living museum with the sea ever close by. As the morning sun lights up the marble, there's a tangible sense of stepping through time, undisturbed by modern noise. It's a must to bring good footwear and a sense of wonder when exploring this grand, weather-worn boulevard.

The Roman Theatre

Tucked against the forested hillside, Phaselis' Roman theatre is a silent amphitheatre of stone, once filled with music, drama, and communal gatherings. Built in the 2nd century AD, this 1,500-seat semi-circular structure overlooks the sea and blends beautifully into the natural slope of the terrain. Climbing its stone steps offers not just a view of the stage, but a sweeping vista of forest, ruins, and coast. It's a perfect place to pause, take photos, and reflect on the cultural life of the ancients who once called this place home. With no modern construction disturbing the surroundings, the site evokes an intimacy that large city ruins often lack.

The Hadrian Waterway Gate

Marking the entrance from the city's main road toward the sea, the Hadrian Waterway Gate stands in honour of Emperor Hadrian's visit in 129 AD. Though partially in ruins, its elegant Roman architecture and surviving inscriptions still tell a vivid story of imperial presence and civic pride. Visitors are drawn to its quiet grandeur and the thought of emperors once passing through these arches on their Mediterranean tours. It's a poignant place to photograph or sit in contemplation as pine trees sway gently overhead. This arch is both a literal and symbolic gateway into the legacy of a city that embraced both East and West.

The Agora and Baths Complex

Near the southern harbour, the remains of the agora and adjoining Roman bathhouses reveal how the people of Phaselis lived, traded, and socialised. The large open courtyard of the agora, surrounded by ruined pillars and stone stalls, once bustled with market activity and political debate. Nearby, the bath complex, with its hypocaust system still visible, speaks of Roman engineering and the culture of leisure. Exploring this area gives insight into the rhythms of ancient daily life—practical, sophisticated, and deeply communal. With moss-draped stonework and the distant sound of waves, it's a setting that feeds both historical curiosity and imagination.

The Three Harbours

Phaselis was uniquely positioned with three natural harbours—Northern, Central, and Southern—making it a maritime marvel of its age and a favourite of seafarers. Today, these calm, turquoise inlets remain breathtakingly beautiful and perfect for swimming, kayaking, or picnicking along the shore. Boats still drop anchor here, just as they did over two thousand years ago, allowing visitors to arrive the way the ancients once did. The clarity of the water, set against crumbling stone jetties and forested headlands, makes this site one of the most photogenic in all of Antalya. No other archaeological site in the region offers such a seamless blend of history and seafront relaxation.

4.9 Perge Ancient City

Perge Ancient City stands as a monumental testament to Anatolia's layered civilizations, echoing through the ruins of what was once a thriving Hellenistic-Roman metropolis. This archaeological jewel, located around 17 kilometres east of Antalya city centre in the Aksu district, is easily accessed by bus, tram, or private taxi. Known for its symmetry, scale, and extraordinary state of preservation, Perge offers more than just stone and silence—it offers a vivid glimpse into how the ancients lived, governed, worshipped, and celebrated life. Entry fees are modest and well justified, typically around 340 Turkish Lira, with Museum Pass options available.

The Roman Theatre of Perge

This semi-circular marvel just outside the city walls once held up to 15,000 spectators, an astonishing feat of ancient engineering and social organisation. Carved reliefs of mythological scenes still adorn the stage area, portraying Dionysian dramas once performed under open skies. Located at the entrance of Perge, it is one of the first grand sights a visitor encounters and sets the tone for the awe that follows. Though partially ruined, its tiered seating and arched corridors remain largely intact, inviting visitors to climb, sit and imagine the roaring applause of Roman crowds. It's a perfect introduction to how entertainment, culture, and political life intertwined in Perge's golden age.

The Hellenistic Gate and City Walls

The twin towers of the Hellenistic Gate, built in the 3rd century BCE, form an arresting entry point into the heart of ancient Perge and once stood as a powerful symbol of the city's defence and civic pride. The gate's round towers are linked by a wide courtyard that was later converted into a Roman nymphaeum, adding layers of history to its original function. Situated just beyond the ticket booth and information area, this area is often where guided tours begin, and rightly so—it's a visual narrative in stone. As you step through the gates, the sudden expansion into the colonnaded avenue gives the feeling of being swallowed by a long-lost world. This space sets the stage for the architectural harmony and order that defines the city.

The Colonnaded Street and Water Canal

Stretching over 300 metres, the main avenue of Perge is flanked by rows of Ionic and Corinthian columns, their bases still solidly rooted in the stone pavements that once carried sandal-clad citizens. A marble-paved water canal runs through its centre, once used for both function and show—reflecting sunlight during the day and the stars at night. Visitors will find this area just past the Hellenistic Gate, heading straight towards the agora and baths, a corridor that would have hosted traders, philosophers, and politicians. It's a scene that evokes not just admiration but connection—you walk where thousands did before, amidst their markets and discussions. The street is perfect for photographs, but also for deep reflection on human civilization's ingenuity.

The Roman Bath Complex

Built in the 2nd century AD and one of the best-preserved ruins within Perge, the Roman baths offer an architectural and social lesson in one glance. Located just north of the colonnaded street and easily identified by its wide arched chambers, the baths were more than hygiene facilities—they were communal hubs of diplomacy and relaxation. Here, one can understand how Roman life balanced luxury with daily necessity, a lesson in the power of civic infrastructure. The complex also provides shaded areas ideal for cooling off after a hot Antalya afternoon.

The Agora (Marketplace)

Tucked beside the baths and near the palaestra, the ancient agora of Perge was the city's commercial and social nucleus, where merchants traded silks, spices, and stories. This large open courtyard, once lined with shops and encircled by a stoa, allows visitors to grasp the economic sophistication of Roman Perge. Though most of its walls have crumbled, the layout is unmistakable and impressively symmetrical, a feature that still inspires urban planners today. It's an ideal place to sit and ponder the rhythms of ancient daily life, where business, gossip, and community thrived in the open air.

4.10 Aspendos Theatre

Located around 45 kilometres east of Antalya city centre, the Aspendos Theatre Can be reached easily by car, tour bus, or local dolmuş minibus services. The entry fee is generally about 340 Turkish Lira, or free with a valid Museum Pass, and the ticket also grants access to surrounding ruins. This site is far more than a shell of antiquity—it is an active stage of memory, where ancient voices echo beneath the Mediterranean sky.

The Main Theatre Structure
The theatre itself is the crown jewel of Aspendos, built during Emperor Marcus Aurelius' reign and seating nearly 15,000 spectators in a perfect semicircle. Its tiered seating, soaring scaenae frons (stage backdrop), and acoustic perfection remain unrivalled, with performances still held here today under moonlit skies. Located directly at the site's main entrance, this theatre reveals its full grandeur

only once inside, where scale and craftsmanship overwhelm the senses. The structure was designed by the local architect Zenon and is a marvel of Roman engineering, preserved almost entirely in its original form. Visitors can wander freely across the marble rows, climb the upper levels, or stand centre stage, whispering into the past.

The Stage and Orchestra Pit

Positioned directly in front of the stage building, the orchestra area was once the beating heart of dramatic performances and musical spectacles. The semi-circular pit still holds remnants of marble flooring and channels that directed rainwater away, proving Roman mastery over both art and utility. It's a space that invites visitors to pause and envision actors in togas performing tragedies or flutes and lyres rising in harmony. While the seating above offers a grand view, standing in the orchestra pit gives a sense of participation and proximity to the performance. This is where you sense the pulse of Roman cultural life, frozen yet alive within the stone.

The Stage Façade and Backstage Chambers

The vertical splendour of the stage façade, still soaring to full height, is adorned with Corinthian columns, niches, and carvings, a visual symphony of Roman artistic expression. Accessible from the lower end of the seating tiers, these areas allow visitors to imagine the bustle behind the curtains—choruses warming up, props being hauled, scripts whispered in dim corridors. The craftsmanship here is unmatched, with each decorative relief serving as both ornament and homage to myth and empire. It's an ideal corner for lovers of art, performance, and hidden layers of history.

The Upper Gallery and Archways

Rising above the seating area, the upper gallery and arched passageways demonstrate how Roman architecture could combine beauty with crowd control and ventilation. From this level, accessible via stone staircases on both sides, one can admire sweeping views of the theatre below and the countryside beyond. These vaulted corridors once housed vendors and mingling spectators, buzzing with excitement before a performance began. The engineering here also allowed perfect sound to reach every corner, with arches acting like amplifiers to the spoken word. For photographers and romantics alike, this high perch offers a timeless vista and unmatched perspective of both structure and setting.

The Aqueduct and Surrounding Ruins

Just beyond the theatre, an ancient aqueduct snakes across the nearby hills—part of a water system that once sustained the city of Aspendos, showcasing Roman infrastructure at its most practical and grand. Though lesser known than the theatre, these aqueduct remains are an essential part of the site and worth exploring by foot for a full appreciation of Aspendos' former scale. The ruins are scattered across an open field behind the theatre, where fragments of basilicas, agora foundations, and city gates whisper of civic life long faded. This area adds depth to the experience, connecting entertainment, urban planning, and survival in one historical sweep. Walking here in the golden light of late afternoon evokes a world where empires didn't just entertain, they thrived.

4.11 Guided Tours and Recommended Tour Operators

Antalya's sun-drenched coastline and ancient ruins come alive when explored with knowledgeable guides who blend local insight with seamless logistics. Whether you crave the mythology of Perge, the cascading beauty of Düden Waterfalls or the hidden coves along the Mediterranean, choosing the right operator shapes every moment of your journey. From private chauffeured excursions to small-group cultural treks, Antalya's tour companies cater to every pace and passion.

Antalya Classic Hotel & Travel

Offering daily excursions through Antalya's historical and natural wonders, Antalya Classic Hotel & Travel excels at blending comfort with authenticity. Their website, https://www.classic-hotel-travel.com, details half- and full-day tours to Perge, Aspendos, Termessos and the Düden Waterfalls. Guests benefit from English, German and Russian–speaking guides, air-conditioned vehicles and flexible pick-up from any Antalya hotel or port. Pricing starts at €45 per person for group tours, with private options available upon request, and free cancellation up to 24 hours in advance. Travelers praise the company's punctuality, local insights and personalized service.

Filika Travel

Filika Travel specializes in bespoke private tours along Antalya's coastline and hinterland, combining archaeological sites with authentic culinary experiences. Visit https://filikatravel.com to explore tailor-made itineraries, from romantic yacht charters to full-day Cappadocia excursions. Their multilingual guides—fluent in English, Spanish and Arabic—ensure every cultural nuance is communicated with clarity. All tours include entrance fees, bottled water, hotel transfers and complimentary travel insurance for peace of mind. Bookings can be confirmed instantly online, with 24-hour support for last-minute changes or special requests.

Tour About Turkey
Renowned for small-group explorations, Tour About Turkey offers immersive discoveries of Antalya's Roman heritage and coastal splendors via https://www.touraboutturkey.com. Their curated packages cover ancient cities like Myra, the sunken church at Simena and the Lycian Way, led by certified archaeologists and local historians. Comfortable minibuses, light snacks and professional photography services are standard inclusions, ensuring an engaging yet relaxed pace. Tour prices begin at $60 per person, inclusive of all museum and site admissions, and seasonal discounts apply. Flexible departure times and multilingual commentary elevate each journey's depth.

Natureland Tour
Natureland Tour focuses on eco-friendly adventures through Antalya's natural landscapes, combining hiking, rafting and jeep safaris in one seamless experience. Details of their sustainable itineraries appear at https://www.naturelandtour.com, where you'll find half-day canyon rafting trips in Köprülü Canyon National Park and full-day mountain treks to Mount Tahtalı. Professional guides equipped with first-aid training lead groups no larger than twelve, ensuring safety and minimal environmental impact. Transfers from Antalya city center, packed vegan-friendly lunches and all necessary equipment are included. Bookings require a 20% deposit, refundable up to 48 hours before departure.

Travelshop Turkey
As a longstanding travel agency in Antalya, Travelshop Turkey offers extensive day tours alongside airport transfers, private cruises and cultural workshops via https://www.travelshopturkey.com. Their signature Antalya Old Town walking tour pairs Ottoman history with hands-on craft sessions led by local artisans. All excursions are customizable, boasting licensed guides fluent in English, French and Italian, plus complimentary pick-up/drop-off service. Tour fees start from €35 per person for standard group outings, with VIP upgrades available for private vehicles and gourmet lunch options. Customer support is available 24/7 via live chat and WhatsApp.

CHAPTER 5
PRACTICAL INFORMATION AND GUIDANCE

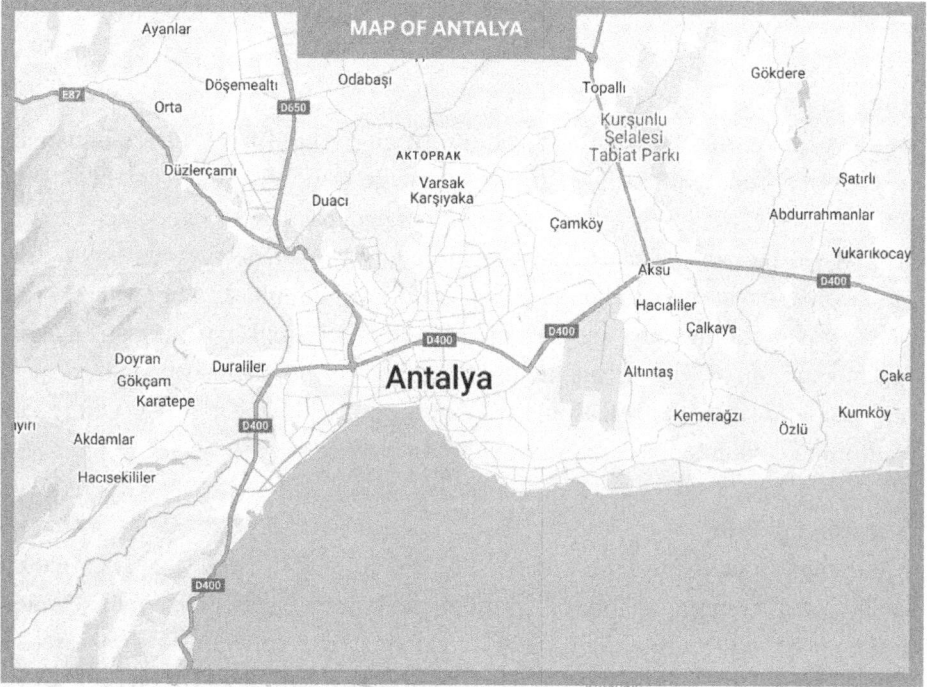

SCAN THE QR CODE WITH A DEVICE TO VIEW COMPREHENSIVE
AND LARGER MAP OF ANTALYA

5.1 Maps and Navigation

Antalya demands an astute sense of direction for travellers wishing to truly immerse themselves. Whether one's journey leads to the winding alleys of Kaleiçi or the far-flung ruins of Termessos, navigating efficiently is essential. Thankfully, Antalya offers a range of mapping resources both in traditional formats and through modern digital channels that cater to visitors of all kinds. Understanding how best to access and use these tools can significantly elevate the quality of a trip.

Antalya Tourist Map

For those who prefer the tactile assurance of a paper map, Antalya does not disappoint. Printed tourist maps are widely available across the city, most notably at the airport's tourist information counters, major hotels, central bus terminals, and inside the old town's information kiosks. These maps are usually free, clearly marked with essential landmarks, and often come annotated with walking trails, museum locations, tram routes, and historical highlights. Many versions are bilingual, combining English and Turkish, which proves useful when asking locals for directions using map references.

Digital Maps for Modern-Day Wanderers

Technology has transformed the traveller's experience, and nowhere is this more evident than in how we navigate cities like Antalya. Applications such as Google Maps, Maps.me, Apple Maps, and Here WeGo provide dynamic, interactive guides to the city's maze of streets, coastlines, and transit systems. With GPS-enabled navigation, users can find precise walking or driving directions to everything from a local beach café to a remote archaeological site in the Taurus Mountains. These apps also allow for public transport mapping, which is indispensable when deciphering Antalya's tram and dolmuş networks.

Offline Digital Navigation and How to Prepare for It

Despite the ease of internet access in Antalya, certain areas—particularly rural archaeological zones—can experience poor connectivity. Savvy travellers are advised to download offline maps before venturing out. Google Maps allows for area downloads, while Maps.me functions entirely offline after initial setup, proving incredibly useful when roaming fees or signal loss becomes a concern. It's best to update these downloads before leaving Wi-Fi zones in your accommodation or local cafés, ensuring that even without mobile data, navigation remains reliable and uninterrupted.

How and Where to Access Printed Maps On Arrival

Upon arriving in Antalya, visitors can locate printed maps not only at the airport but also inside city-run tourist information centres, which are strategically located at Kaleiçi Marina, Republic Square, and near the Antalya Museum entrance. These maps are usually provided with updated content for the current tourist season, and the attendants often point out hidden gems that are not easily found online. Hotels, particularly those in the mid-range to upscale categories, also keep a stock of pocket-sized city maps at their front desks for guests' convenience.

Instant Access Through QR Code and Web Link Provided

For ease and efficiency, readers of this guide are encouraged to access an exclusive, curated digital map of Antalya. By clicking the link or scanning the QR code included in this book, travellers can open a dynamic, mobile-friendly version of Antalya's full map. This digital resource is interactive and updated regularly to reflect road changes, new attractions, and revised opening hours, allowing users to bookmark locations, plan routes, and toggle between street and satellite views. It is an indispensable companion to both spontaneous exploration and structured itineraries.

Navigating With Public Transit Maps and Signage

Antalya's public transit network is easy to use, but only if you understand its layout. Trams, city buses, and local minibuses operate on scheduled routes that are posted at stops and terminals, but not all signage is in English. Downloadable transit maps, which are available via the Antalya Municipality's transport portal or accessible through apps like Moovit, can be invaluable. Paper-based transit maps can also be picked up at major terminals such as Otogar (Main Bus Station) and are often integrated into general tourist maps to show the proximity of landmarks to tram stops.

Using Maps to Enhance Cultural Discovery

With a detailed map in hand, either digital or printed, visitors can uncover smaller, lesser-known sights that may not make it to guide books—such as tucked-away Ottoman fountains, forgotten Lycian tombs, or the best local spots for simit and tea. Using maps as a tool for deeper exploration rather than mere direction-finding adds a richer dimension to travel. It transforms the experience from simple sightseeing to genuine discovery, grounded in context and curiosity.

5.2 Essential Packing List

Antalya's Mediterranean, meaning hot summers, mild winters, and plenty of sunshine year-round. Visitors should anticipate significant UV exposure, especially from late spring to early autumn. This calls for a packing strategy that prioritizes lightweight and breathable fabrics with adequate sun protection. Understanding the city's geography also helps in packing sensibly for both coastal and inland excursions.

Clothing Essentials for Comfort and Modesty

Antalya's relaxed yet traditional atmosphere means clothing should be both functional and culturally respectful. While beachwear is acceptable along the coast, more modest attire is expected in mosques, villages, and traditional marketplaces. Loose cotton shirts, light trousers, and knee-length skirts are ideal for maintaining comfort in the heat. Evening outings, particularly in upscale venues, may require something slightly more formal or refined.

Footwear Suitable for Varied Terrains

Antalya's cobbled streets, hiking trails, and beachfront promenades demand practical footwear. Sandals with good support work well for daily walks, but sturdier hiking shoes are essential for excursions to ancient ruins like Termessos or treks in the Beydağları Mountains. Flip-flops are convenient for hotel pools and beach days but not suited for long walks. Many historical sites require walking over uneven stones and steps, so comfort and grip are vital. If visiting religious sites, easy-to-remove shoes are also a good idea.

Protection Against the Elements

Though Antalya is synonymous with sunshine, it is still wise to prepare for occasional changes in weather and natural conditions. A foldable umbrella or light raincoat can come in handy during unpredictable spring showers or autumn drizzles. Sunscreen with a high SPF, lip balm with UV protection, and after-sun lotion are indispensable during summer. Reusable water bottles are also critical to stay hydrated in the heat. Insect repellent will offer relief in coastal or garden areas, especially in humid evenings.

Swimming and Water Gear Necessities

With its alluring turquoise coastline, Antalya practically demands time in the sea, so visitors should pack accordingly. A swimsuit or two, microfiber travel towels, and water shoes for rocky beaches or boat trips are must-haves.

Snorkeling enthusiasts may prefer to bring their own gear for hygiene and comfort, especially when venturing to less crowded coves. Waterproof pouches will protect valuables while swimming or during waterfall visits. Those planning water sports might consider rash guards or protective clothing for prolonged exposure.

Technology and Travel Accessories
To make the most of modern conveniences, travelers should not overlook essential gadgets and accessories. A universal plug adapter is a necessity as Turkey uses the Europlug (Type C, 220V). Portable power banks help ensure smartphones and cameras stay charged for mapping, translation, and photography. Digital maps and travel apps can ease navigation in the city and its outskirts. Offline backups of key travel documents should be stored both on devices and in printed copies. Noise-cancelling headphones are a blessing for long bus or flight journeys.

Health, Hygiene, and First Aid Items
Maintaining hygiene and being prepared for minor ailments should not be an afterthought when heading to Antalya. Hand sanitizer, antibacterial wipes, and personal hygiene products offer reassurance, particularly during long outings. Basic medication such as painkillers, antihistamines, and travel sickness tablets should be brought along, especially for those planning boat tours. A mini first-aid kit with plasters, antiseptic cream, and tweezers can be invaluable in remote areas. Those with specific medical conditions should carry prescriptions and doctor's notes as a precaution.

Documents, Currency, and Local Essentials
Travelers should ensure that all required documentation is safely stored yet accessible. This includes passports, visas if applicable, hotel confirmations, and insurance papers. A money belt or concealed pouch provides an extra layer of security in crowded areas. Turkish phrasebooks or downloaded translation apps can be a lifeline in rural settings where English may not be spoken. It also helps to have physical copies of transport timetables or attraction maps.

Seasonal Adaptations and Trip Planning
The time of year heavily influences what needs to be packed, and wise travelers prepare accordingly. In the summer, lighter fabrics, sun gear, and hydration aids take priority. Autumn and spring invite more variation, requiring layering

options and occasional rain gear. Winter, though mild, can still warrant jackets, closed shoes, and heavier trousers, especially inland or during mountain excursions. Festivals or religious events might also demand more traditional or formal attire. Customizing the packing list by season ensures one is never caught off guard while exploring this diverse and historic region.

5.3 Setting Your Travel Budget

Setting a realistic travel budget is the cornerstone of any successful trip, and when planning a visit to Antalya, getting your finances in order can be the difference between a stress-free experience and an unexpected strain. Understanding the costs behind these experiences ensures a traveller avoids last-minute shocks. Budgeting isn't simply about restriction but about enabling choice and flexibility across accommodations, meals, and activities. With good planning, Antalya becomes more than a postcard-perfect escape—it becomes a journey that's smart, fulfilling, and within means.

Accommodation Costs and Seasonal Influence

Where you choose to rest your head in Antalya greatly affects your overall expenditure, and the wide variety of lodging options reflects this. Travellers on a modest budget can find comfortable pensions and hostels, while those seeking indulgence have no shortage of five-star resorts and boutique hotels along the coast. The time of year drastically influences prices, with peak seasons such as July and August seeing a surge in room rates, especially in beachside areas like Lara and Konyaaltı. Booking in advance, particularly in shoulder seasons like May or September, can offer substantial savings without compromising on weather or atmosphere. It's essential to note that many hotels include breakfast in the room rate, offering one less meal to account for in your daily spending.

Transportation Expenses Within and Around the City

Navigating Antalya is cost-effective if approached wisely, and transport options range from modern trams and city buses to taxis and rental cars. The public tram system offers reliable and affordable access to many of the city's key sights, including the museum, Kaleiçi, and the shopping districts. Taxis, while convenient, can be more expensive, particularly during heavy traffic or longer distances like to the airport or ancient cities such as Perge. Car rentals can be practical for exploring areas beyond the city limits, though fuel and insurance should be factored into the budget. For cost-conscious travellers, acquiring an

AntalyaKart—a reloadable transit card—can reduce overall expenses and streamline local movement.

Meals, Dining Out, and Culinary Budgeting

The culinary scene in Antalya provides a chance to experience Turkish cuisine without draining your wallet, but how and where you choose to dine will directly impact your travel budget. Street food such as simit, gözleme, or döner can be found for mere coins, offering authentic and filling options for those on a budget. Mid-range restaurants serving mezes and grilled meats present good value, especially those away from high-traffic tourist zones, which tend to be priced higher. For visitors willing to splurge, fine-dining establishments with sea views are available, but come with premium costs that require advanced budgeting. Many eateries offer set lunch menus at discounted rates, making midday meals a smart place to cut costs without sacrificing taste.

Attractions, Tours, and Entry Fees

Exploring the cultural and historical wonders of Antalya comes with both free and paid opportunities, and careful planning ensures that you get the most out of your sightseeing without overspending. Attractions like the Old Town of Kaleiçi, the Roman Harbour, and beaches are free to wander, but sites like the Antalya Museum, Termessos, or Aspendos Theatre require entry tickets, some of which can be bundled into discounted passes. Guided tours, whether around ancient ruins or through natural sites like the Düden Waterfalls, offer expert insights but come at a cost that should be anticipated ahead. Booking tours online or through local agencies may result in savings when compared to hotel desk rates. It is wise to mix self-guided exploration with selected paid experiences for a well-balanced itinerary.

Shopping, Souvenirs, and Unexpected Costs

One aspect that catches many visitors off guard is the impulse to shop, as Antalya's bazaars, boutiques, and markets brim with textiles, ceramics, jewellery, and spices that are hard to resist. While bargaining is a common practice in many local markets, especially in Kaleiçi, it's easy to overspend without clear boundaries in mind. Additionally, small costs such as bottled water, suncream, tips for service staff, or emergency purchases like medications or clothing replacements can accumulate quickly. Travel insurance, often overlooked, is another necessary cost to safeguard against unforeseen events and should be included in the initial budgeting process. By setting aside a buffer amount for such extras, travellers remain prepared rather than financially stretched.

Currency Exchange and Managing Daily Spending

Antalya operates on the Turkish Lira, and understanding how to handle currency exchange and spending can influence your overall experience and financial comfort. While international credit and debit cards are widely accepted in hotels, larger restaurants, and shops, having cash on hand is essential for public transport, street vendors, and smaller local businesses. Currency can be exchanged at the airport, banks, or licensed exchange bureaus, though rates often vary, and it's worth comparing before committing. Using ATMs is convenient, but it's important to verify international fees with your bank before travel. Keeping track of daily spending—either manually or through travel budgeting apps—helps maintain control and avoids the all-too-common surprise of overspending by the end of the trip.

5.4 Visa Requirements and Entry Procedures

Antalya welcomes millions of visitors annually, but every journey to this historic city begins with understanding the visa and entry protocols set by the Turkish government. These rules are not merely formalities but binding legal requirements that determine who may enter, for how long, and under what circumstances. While Turkey maintains a relatively open-door policy to many countries, especially for short-term tourism, the specifics can vary widely depending on your nationality.

Visa Requirements Based on Nationality

Turkey offers visa-free access to citizens of several countries, allowing them to stay in Antalya for up to 90 days within any 180-day period, provided their purpose is tourism or business. For others, the country's user-friendly e-visa system allows online applications in advance of travel, offering a convenient and often rapid approval process. Applicants generally need a passport valid for at least six months from the date of arrival, along with a credit card and basic travel details. However, citizens of countries not covered by these simplified options must apply for a visa through the nearest Turkish consulate or embassy, which entails a more thorough vetting process, often including an interview and additional documentation.

Arrival by Air and the Airport Entry Process

Antalya Airport serves as the primary international gateway to the city and is well equipped with modern immigration and customs facilities. Upon disembarkation, passengers are directed to passport control where visas—either stamped in advance or presented as an e-visa printout—are verified. Officers may request to see return flight bookings, hotel reservations, or proof of funds. Though many arrivals experience a smooth transition, Turkish border control is strict in applying the rules, especially for those with incomplete or questionable documentation. A limited number of nationalities may still access visas on arrival, but this practice is being phased out in favour of pre-approved digital visas.

Crossing into Antalya by Road or Train

Though Antalya lacks a direct international train station, overland access is possible via road or a combination of train and bus routes, particularly from neighbouring countries. Land border crossings into Turkey are controlled by immigration and customs posts, often busy during peak travel seasons. Drivers must carry valid international driving permits, vehicle registration documents, and cross-border insurance accepted by Turkish authorities. Train travellers typically enter Turkey via Istanbul, continuing their journey south to Antalya using internal rail or bus networks. Regardless of mode, travellers must meet all visa requirements and be prepared for full border checks at the point of entry.

Overstaying and Visa Compliance Concerns

Turkey operates a digital immigration system that records all entries and exits, making it easy for authorities to detect overstays. Those who exceed their visa duration, even by a day, may face monetary fines, mandatory deportation, or even bans on future travel to Turkey. Extensions are rarely granted for tourist visas, and visitors are expected to respect their visa terms strictly. Antalya's immigration office can assist with visa extensions or residency permits, but these applications must be lodged before a visa expires. Ignorance of the rules is not considered a valid excuse, and the consequences for violations can be serious and long-lasting.

Long-Stay Visas and Special Entry Conditions

These visas require more complex documentation, such as sponsorship letters, official acceptance into educational programmes, employment contracts, or proof of family ties. Many also require applicants to hold comprehensive health insurance valid in Turkey for the entire duration of their stay. Once in Antalya, visa holders must register their presence with local authorities and carry identification at all times. Failure to comply with these rules can result in detention, fines, or enforced removal from the country.

5.5 Safety Tips and Emergency Contacts

Staying safe in Antalya requires foresight and awareness. While the region is generally secure and friendly, tourists must remain alert in crowded areas, on public transport, and while exploring remote sites. Understanding local emergency procedures is essential, as swift communication can mean the difference between a minor issue and a serious complication. Whether you're enjoying the historical old town, trekking through the Taurus Mountains, or swimming along the turquoise coast, knowing whom to contact in distress is as important as carrying your passport.

General Emergency Number: 112

The unified emergency number 112 in Turkey is the quickest way to reach help in any crisis, be it medical, fire-related, or criminal. When dialled, the operator connects you to the appropriate department depending on your need, and services are available in English for tourists. This number is operational 24/7 and works from all Turkish mobile and landline providers without the need for a local SIM. In major cities like Antalya, response times are generally fast, particularly for accidents and medical emergencies. Always provide your exact location, preferably a landmark or GPS coordinate, for a faster dispatch.

Antalya Tourist Police

The Antalya Tourist Police are stationed in key tourist districts, especially around Kaleiçi and the central marina, and are trained to assist foreigners. They specialise in handling lost passports, scams, petty theft, and legal troubles affecting visitors. Communication in English is generally smooth, and officers are distinguishable by their badges reading "Turizm Polisi". Their presence is most visible during summer when visitor numbers peak, and you can approach them directly at their booth or call through the local police line. You are encouraged to keep a digital and printed copy of your ID and travel insurance for any report.

Antalya Fire Department

Fires, both structural and wild, are not uncommon during the dry season, especially around the forested outskirts and rural villages. In the event of a fire, dial 112 and ask for the fire brigade; fire stations in Antalya are well-equipped and respond swiftly to urban and resort-related incidents. Firefighters are located across the city, including stations near Konyaaltı, Muratpaşa, and Lara, ensuring area-wide coverage. You can flag down emergency vehicles if they are in sight, or reach out through resort staff for instant coordination. Always obey evacuation instructions and move to designated safe zones when alerted.

Antalya Ambulance Services
Medical assistance in Antalya is highly organised, with both public and private ambulance services operating round-the-clock. Dialling 112 is the most direct way to summon an ambulance, and operators will prioritise calls depending on severity, dispatching the nearest available unit. Most medics speak basic English, especially in tourist hubs, and ambulances carry advanced equipment for trauma and cardiac emergencies. In resorts and hotels, concierge staff can also arrange rapid contact with ambulance units, particularly for non-critical cases. Always have your travel insurance number ready for smoother hospital admission.

Coast Guard and Marine Rescue
Given Antalya's sprawling coastline and its popularity for boating, jet skiing, and diving, the Turkish Coast Guard plays a crucial role in maritime safety. For emergencies at sea, such as capsized vessels or swimmers in distress, you should dial 158, the dedicated number for maritime rescue. Patrol boats are stationed at main harbours like Antalya Marina and Kemer, allowing quick deployment. Resorts and tour operators often have direct lines with the Coast Guard, especially those offering marine excursions. It's advised to check sea conditions and emergency response plans before heading out on water activities.

Antalya Hospitals and Emergency Clinics
The city is well-served by state hospitals like Antalya Training and Research Hospital, as well as reputable private clinics such as Anadolu Hastanesi and Akdeniz Şifa. Most major hospitals have emergency wards operating 24/7 with translators on-call for international patients. Upon arrival, patients are triaged and treated based on urgency, with private clinics offering shorter waiting times for those with travel insurance. Taxi drivers are generally familiar with hospital names and can get you there fast if needed. Make sure to keep your passport and insurance policy number within reach during admittance.

Antalya Earthquake Response

Although not frequent, Antalya lies within a seismically active region, and basic earthquake preparedness is recommended. In the event of tremors, stay clear of glass windows, avoid elevators, and move to open areas or follow signage to evacuation points. The Disaster and Emergency Management Authority (AFAD) coordinates earthquake response and can be contacted via 122. Emergency shelters are designated by the municipality, and locals are usually quick to offer guidance in times of confusion. Aftershocks may follow, so always stay updated via hotel reception or local media channels.

Emergency Consular Assistance

Foreign visitors who lose their passports, face legal issues, or encounter serious personal emergencies should promptly contact their respective consulates in Antalya. While not all countries have embassies in the city, most maintain regional representatives or offer services via consulates in nearby cities like Istanbul. For immediate consular help, call your embassy's emergency number found in your passport or online; they can coordinate with Turkish authorities on your behalf. Consular staff can assist in securing temporary travel documents, legal support, and communication with family back home.

Natural Hazards and Seasonal Alerts

From sudden flash floods in winter to forest fire warnings in summer, Antalya is no stranger to natural events. Pay attention to municipal alerts, which are usually broadcast over radio, hotel notice boards, or public loudspeakers in Turkish and sometimes English. Always avoid hiking in the mountains during storm alerts or extreme heat, as rescue services may be delayed in remote areas. Respect closures and posted warnings on hiking paths and coastal cliffs.

5.6 Currency Exchange and Banking Services

Travelling through Antalya requires familiarity with the local financial systems, especially for visitors managing daily transactions or settling longer stays. The official currency used throughout the city is the Turkish Lira, which is denoted by the symbol ₺ and the ISO code TRY. While some large establishments accept euros or US dollars, local vendors, smaller restaurants and taxis prefer lira, making currency exchange essential. Antalya hosts a robust mix of exchange offices and banks, easily accessible across central districts, airport terminals and tourist hotspots..

DenizBank Currency Exchange Services

Situated within the historic Kaleiçi quarter, DenizBank offers convenient exchange services alongside standard banking operations for travellers. Known for its English-speaking staff and clear digital rate boards, this branch accommodates walk-in clients without requiring an account. It is open weekdays and offers extended hours during peak tourism months, particularly in summer. Its location makes it a favoured stop for tourists exploring Hadrian's Gate or Mermerli Beach. For added security, transactions above a certain threshold require valid identification, usually a passport.

Albaraka Türk Exchange Office

Inside the popular MarkAntalya shopping centre, Albaraka Türk operates a full-service booth that handles major international currencies with transparency. Tourists find this location ideal due to its proximity to fashion retailers and food courts, allowing them to combine errands conveniently. Operating every day, including weekends, this branch ensures reliable exchange even when banks are closed. Customers can opt for receipt-verified exchanges, ensuring clarity in every transaction.

Ziraat Bankas

Found along the busy Lara Boulevard, Ziraat Bankası provides comprehensive banking services including currency exchange, international transfers, and ATM withdrawals. One of Turkey's oldest state-owned institutions, it offers trustworthy rates and allows card-linked services for foreign bank users. The branch maintains a formal atmosphere with ticket-based queues and secure teller systems, offering privacy during transactions. Foreign exchange is processed quickly, but visitors are advised to carry identification and be aware of daily limits. ATMs outside the building offer 24-hour service and support English-language menus.

Garanti BBVA

Garanti BBVA, positioned near Antalya's scenic Konyaaltı Beach, supports tourists with both banking and competitive exchange options. The branch has earned praise for its efficient services, English-speaking tellers, and well-structured premises tailored to accommodate international visitors. It allows foreign debit or credit card cash withdrawals in lira, which can sometimes yield better exchange rates than physical currency conversion. Accessible during extended business hours on weekdays, it also provides online currency calculators for visitors planning ahead. Security is a priority, with monitored entrances and ATM coverage throughout the day.

Doviz Express Currency Exchange

Located in both terminals of Antalya International Airport, Doviz Express is often the first and last stop for visitors requiring currency exchange. While airport exchange points typically offer less favourable rates than city offices, this provider has built a reputation for reliability and immediate access upon arrival. With multi-language support and high cash turnover, it handles large exchanges and rarely runs short on major currencies. The convenience of its location justifies minor differences in rate, particularly for travellers needing local cash for transport or tipping. Service is available around the clock for flights arriving at any hour.

Isbank (Türkiye İş Bankası)

Isbank holds a prominent location within Antalya's historic district, serving as a go-to option for both tourists and residents needing international banking. This branch offers extensive exchange services, overseas money transfers via SWIFT, and even account services for long-stay travellers or digital nomads. Staff are professionally trained to assist foreigners, and many counters provide assistance in English. The building's classic Turkish design blends well with the area's Ottoman-era charm, drawing the attention of culturally curious visitors.

5.7 Language, Communication and Useful Phrases

Antalya welcomes millions of international visitors each year, and with that comes a rich blend of languages heard on its bustling streets and beaches. While the city retains a strong sense of local culture, its tourism-forward economy ensures that communication barriers are often bridged with hospitality and adaptability. Still, to engage more deeply with locals and navigate daily experiences smoothly, understanding the local language and common communication styles proves highly valuable. A few well-placed Turkish words can elevate a visitor's experience from merely pleasant to memorably authentic.

The Official Language and Its Local Influence

Turkish is the official language of Antalya and is spoken universally across all age groups, in both casual and formal settings. It is a rich, vowel-heavy language rooted in Central Asian linguistic traditions, modernised under Atatürk's reforms using the Latin alphabet. Although English is commonly spoken in tourist zones such as Kaleiçi, Konyaaltı, and Lara Beach, venturing beyond these areas reveals a reliance on Turkish, especially in markets and villages. Hotel staff, tour guides, and restaurant servers often speak multiple languages, but locals in non-touristic spaces typically use only Turkish.

Practical Communication Beyond Language

In Antalya, communication extends beyond words and relies heavily on gestures, facial expressions, and tone. The Turkish custom of respectful and formal address is apparent in daily interactions, where greetings are important and often accompanied by eye contact and a slight nod or handshake. Visitors will find that showing effort in communication, even when limited in vocabulary, is appreciated more than perfection. Bargaining in markets and hailing taxis can often be achieved with a few words, supported by gestures and a smile. Learning to read the cultural cues in tone and mannerisms helps bridge the gap where vocabulary falls short.

Common Turkish Phrases Every Visitor Should Know

Visitors learning certain Turkish phrases helps them establish simple conversation and shows the locals that they appreciate the local culture. A simple "Merhaba" (Hello) or "Teşekkür ederim" (Thank you) is met with genuine warmth, and the ability to say "Lütfen" (Please) or "Afedersiniz" (Excuse me) reflects respect. Asking basic questions like "Ne kadar?" (How much?) is incredibly useful in markets or transport situations. Phrases such as "İngilizce biliyor musunuz?" (Do you speak English?) are handy ice-breakers in unfamiliar areas. Locals admire visitors who try to speak their language, no matter how limited their grasp.

Language Support Services and Translation Tools

Antalya's tourism infrastructure offers a range of support for non-Turkish speakers, from multilingual signage in public transport and major attractions to digital assistance. Hotels and tour agencies often employ English, German, or Russian speakers to accommodate the main visitor demographics. Translation apps like Google Translate function well in Turkey and are widely used in shops or for menu reading. Some larger establishments provide printed menus and brochures in multiple languages, while tourist information centers often have English-speaking staff to assist with navigation and cultural queries. Mobile connectivity is good, so using translation tools on the go rarely poses a problem.

5.8 Shopping in Antalya

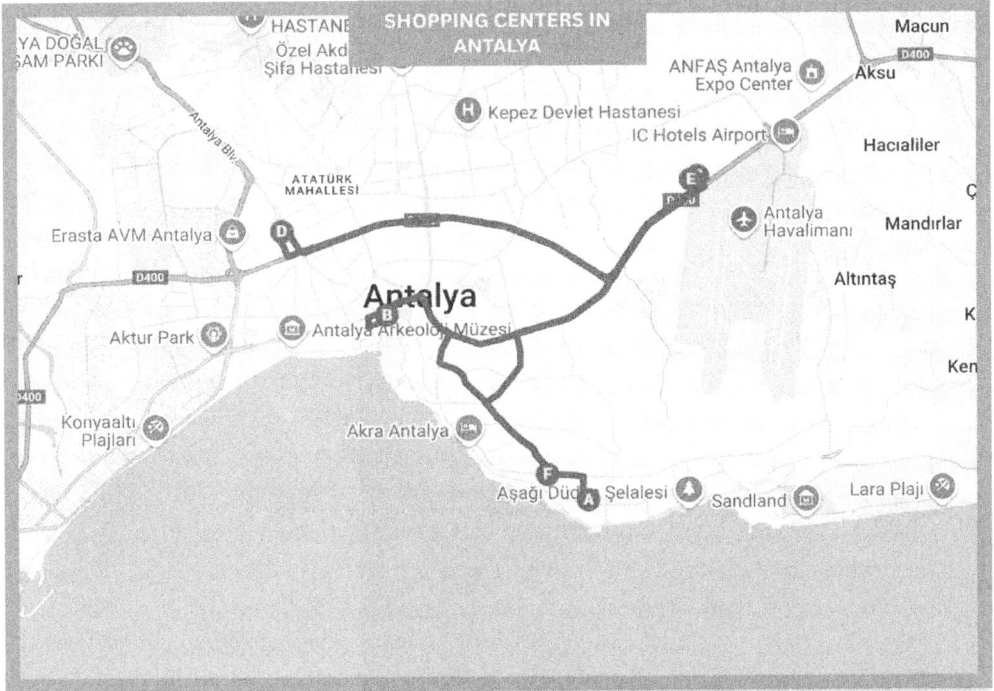

Directions from TerraCity, Fener, Tekelioğlu Caddesi, Muratpaşa/Antalya, Türkiye to Laura Avm, Fener, Bülent Ecevit Bulvarı, Muratpaşa/Antalya, Türkiye

A
TerraCity, Fener, Tekelioğlu Caddesi, Muratpaşa/Antalya, Türkiye

D
ÖzdilekPark Antalya AVM, Fabrikalar, Fikri Erten Caddesi, Kepez/Antalya, Türkiye

B
MarkAntalya Mall, Tahılpazarı, Kazım Özalp Street, Muratpaşa/Antalya, Türkiye

E
Deepo Outlet Center, Altınova Sinan, Serik Street, Kepez/Antalya, Türkiye

C
Mall of Antalya, Mahallesi, Altınova Sinan, Serik Street, Kepez/Antalya, Türkiye

F
Laura Avm, Fener, Bülent Ecevit Bulvarı, Muratpaşa/Antalya, Türkiye

76

Antalya's shopping experience extends well beyond the confines of tourism. It blends modern retail culture with everyday Turkish life, offering both international brand names and local craftsmanship under one roof. Malls here are designed not only as commercial hubs but also as recreational spaces, merging shopping with dining, entertainment, and social interaction. Their strategic locations across the city make them accessible whether you're staying in the historic Kaleiçi district or along the beach resorts.

TerraCity Shopping Centre
Located on Tekelioğlu Caddesi No:55 in the Fener Mahallesi area of Muratpaşa, TerraCity has become one of the most frequented retail spaces in Antalya. With more than 180 stores spread across multiple levels, it caters to those interested in mid- to high-end fashion, tech gadgets, and cosmetics. You'll find both Turkish brands and widely recognized international labels, with clothing prices starting from around 150 TL and rising beyond 600 TL depending on the store. Buses like KL08 and TC93 stop directly at the mall, making it easy to reach from anywhere in the city. The food court upstairs offers a wide selection of eateries, including both Turkish meals and international fast-food options.

MarkAntalya Shopping Complex
Home to more than 150 stores, the mall covers a broad range of shopping needs—from fashion to electronics, accessories to home essentials. Brands such as LC Waikiki, Bershka, and DeFacto are well represented. Most clothing items fall between 200 and 450 TL, making it suitable for both mid-range shoppers and bargain hunters. The tramway stops just outside the entrance, and indoor parking facilities are available. Inside, there are also restaurants, a children's activity zone, and a cinema.

Mall of Antalya
Situated at Serik Caddesi No:309 in the Altınova Sinan Mahallesi of Kepez, Mall of Antalya is one of the city's newest and largest commercial centers. Located only about 10 minutes from Antalya Airport, the mall spans over 130,000 square meters and includes a mix of clothing stores, sporting goods outlets, electronic shops, and homeware retailers. Price ranges vary widely depending on the product, but mid-level fashion generally starts at 250 TL. There's an 11-screen cinema and a large indoor playground for families. Public transport runs frequently to the mall, and hotel shuttles often include it in their routes.

ÖzdilekPark Antalya

Found at Namık Kemal Bulvarı No:5 in the Fabrikalar Mahallesi, ÖzdilekPark is a well-managed retail space that balances local and international offerings. With over 100 shops, the mall features brands like Mango, Colin's, and Park Bravo, alongside local retailers with unique Turkish designs. Product prices can be quite reasonable, with many items available under 300 TL. The nearby Dumka tram stop ensures convenient access, while the clean, organized interior provides a relaxed shopping environment. Besides clothing and electronics, there are also cafes and fast-food restaurants, making it a good place to spend several hours.

Deepo Outlet Center

What sets Deepo apart is its exclusive focus on outlet shopping. With over 90 brand-name outlets, it offers previous-season items from well-known labels like Adidas, Puma, and Levi's at discounted rates. Price reductions often reach up to 70%, making it a favourite for budget-conscious shoppers. City buses like AC03 connect the downtown area to Deepo, and the mall provides ample free parking. Cafés and snack bars are scattered throughout to keep visitors refreshed.

Laura Shopping Centre

Laura AVM sits on Kordonboyu Caddesi No:2 in the Lara section of Konyaaltı and maintains a more relaxed, suburban feel. With about 90 stores, it's more compact than some of the other malls, but still covers essential shopping categories including fashion, personal care, gifts, and local products. Pricing is moderate, with many items in the 100 to 300 TL range. Public buses such as LC07 and KL08 stop just outside, and on-site parking is also available. A cinema, playground, and seasonal exhibitions provide entertainment options, particularly appealing to families and younger visitors.

5.9 Health and Wellness Centers

Antalya has steadily become a destination for individuals seeking holistic health treatments, spa therapies, and rehabilitative care. With access to expert practitioners and diverse healing traditions, visitors can find modern facilities tailored to detox, relaxation, or medical recovery. The following health and wellness centres, all currently in operation, reflect the city's commitment to both body and mind restoration.

TheLifeCo Wellbeing Akra Antalya

Located within the grounds of Akra Hotel, this centre focuses on detoxification and overall wellness using medically guided programmes. Its address is Eski Lara Yolu, Akra Barut & Akra Park, 07100 Muratpaşa, Antalya, easily reached from both the city and airport. Contact can be made through +90 242 316 68 45 or antalya@thelifeco.com for consultation and booking inquiries. Clients typically enrol in structured stays that include fasting, organic nutrition, and emotional well-being sessions. It operates all week with customized options to suit a guest's duration and specific health targets.

Akra Spa & Wellness

This wellness facility is part of the Akra Hotel and boasts expansive space for Turkish hammams, skin care, and traditional massage therapy. It is located on Lara Caddesi No:24 in Muratpaşa, not far from central Antalya or public transport lines. To make a reservation, guests may call +90 242 310 99 99 or email info@akrahotels.com. Guests have access to massage rooms, saunas, and a fully equipped fitness studio with instructor-led sessions. Appointments are encouraged for peak hours, especially for signature therapies and couple treatments.

Vaveyla Spa & Wellness

This centre combines Turkish bathing traditions with contemporary comfort, offering a range of hot therapies and dry salt room sessions. Found at 2348. Sokak No:21 in Güzeloba, Muratpaşa, it is a short drive or taxi ride from Lara's hotel strip. Inquiries and bookings are handled through +90 554 342 49 54 or info@vaveylaspa.com. It operates daily and caters to both international and Turkish guests with emphasis on privacy and sanitation. The treatments here focus on exfoliation, muscle relaxation, and mental reset in a low-noise atmosphere.

Vogue Delux Güzellik Merkezi

This is a beauty and care facility that blends modern salon treatments with relaxing therapies like light massage and body care. Located on Bülent Ecevit Boulevard 27/B in Muratpaşa, it is easy to access via taxi or foot from major downtown hotels. Clients can reach the centre at +90 242 323 34 35 to make an appointment or ask about service options. Popular with both residents and tourists, it is recognised for cleanliness and friendly, English-speaking staff.

Visitors come for everything from facial care and waxing to skin rejuvenation using high-grade products.

Fizyorest Sağlıklı Yaşam Merkezi
This physiotherapy and wellness practice provides recovery-based care using clinical Pilates, rehabilitation massage, and manual therapy. Its address is Atatürk Bulvarı, Efeoğlu Apt. No:68, Daire 1, Konyaaltı, within walking distance of the Konyaaltı beachfront. Health seekers can book appointments through +90 533 464 60 85 or by emailing info@fizyorest.com. Services are handled by licensed therapists with experience in orthopedic and sports-related recovery. Treatment plans can include in-clinic sessions or home visits, tailored to each person's progress and physical limits.

5.10 Useful Websites and Online Resources
Antalya, is a city where history, culture, and modern convenience converge. While the winding alleys of Kaleiçi and the turquoise shores of Konyaaltı Beach transport visitors to another era, the digital age has firmly taken root. For any traveller seeking to navigate this vibrant coastal city, a grasp of the most useful websites, mobile applications, and online platforms is not just an advantage—it is a necessity. These tools do not merely guide; they enable deeper exploration, smoother logistics, and a safer, more informed stay.

The City's Official Tourism Portal
For any visitor wanting verified and up-to-date information, the city's own digital tourism hub, www.visitantalya.com, offers a comprehensive overview of what Antalya has to offer. This official website is managed by the Antalya Metropolitan Municipality and functions as a centralised resource for planning everything from sightseeing and event attendance to understanding the local culture and transportation network. It provides digital brochures, maps, and recommendations, along with seasonal event calendars and travel advisories.

AntalyaKart App – For Public Transport Navigation
Public transport in Antalya is both reliable and cost-effective, but only if you are equipped with the correct tools. The AntalyaKart Mobil application is indispensable for navigating the city's buses and trams. Available on Android and iOS, this app links directly to the city's smart card system and enables users to load funds, check routes, monitor transport schedules, and view nearest bus stops. The corresponding website, www.antalyaulasim.com.tr, works in tandem

with the app, offering live vehicle tracking and fare calculators. Visitors should note that Antalya has gone fully digital in its transport fare system, and cash is no longer accepted on buses or trams, making the AntalyaKart app more than just a convenience—it is a necessity.

Moovit and Trafi – Real-Time Urban Mobility Apps
While the AntalyaKart app is optimal for local transit payments, third-party apps like Moovit and Trafi provide a broader perspective on real-time urban mobility. Moovit, available at www.moovitapp.com, offers route planning, bus arrival times, and disruption alerts in English and other major languages. Trafi works similarly and is available for download via www.trafi.com. These platforms can sometimes outperform local apps when it comes to accuracy and interface simplicity, particularly for non-Turkish speakers.

GetYourGuide and Viator
Those wishing to explore Antalya's rich historical and natural heritage will find that platforms like GetYourGuide (www.getyourguide.com) and Viator (www.viator.com) provide not only convenience but competitive pricing for day trips, museum tickets, boat tours, and guided excursions. These platforms are especially useful for last-minute bookings and include user reviews, digital vouchers, and multi-language customer support. In Antalya, popular tours such as the Lower Duden Waterfalls cruise, ancient city visits to Termessos or Perge, and off-road Taurus mountain safaris are readily available via these services.

Yemeksepeti and Getir
Culinary exploration is a highlight of any visit to Antalya, and for those wishing to enjoy the region's food from the comfort of their hotel or apartment, Yemeksepeti and GetirYemek are the go-to platforms. Yemeksepeti, accessible via www.yemeksepeti.com, is the most widely used food delivery app in Turkey and offers services in English. It covers everything from döner and pide to sushi and vegan options. GetirYemek, a division of the Getir delivery app (www.getir.com), also offers grocery delivery in minutes and operates around the clock in Antalya's central areas. Both platforms accept international credit cards and offer tracking in real time.

Turkish Language Apps and Emergency Services Access
Though English is spoken widely in tourist areas, a Turkish phrasebook app such as Duolingo (www.duolingo.com) or Google Translate with offline Turkish

language pack is highly recommended for seamless communication. Many official emergency services in Antalya, such as police (155), ambulance (112), and fire (110), now operate through the general ALO 112 emergency platform which integrates all services. Their app, called 112 Acil Çağrı, is available on Android and iOS and is useful for both voice calls and location-based alerts in an emergency.

5.11 Internet Access and Connectivity

As a city deeply connected to tourism, Antalya has made notable strides in ensuring stable and fast internet access across all its urban and resort zones. Visitors who rely on seamless digital connectivity for navigation, work, communication, or entertainment will find the city's digital infrastructure reliably serviceable. Digital convenience is integrated into most visitor experiences, making staying online in Antalya hassle-free.

Public Wifi In Urban And Tourist Areas

Internet access in Antalya is widely available through public Wi-Fi hotspots scattered across high-traffic zones, including major parks, public transport terminals, shopping malls, and beachfront promenades. These connections are usually provided by the local municipality or commercial outlets seeking to enhance customer experience. While these networks are often free, users may be required to log in with a Turkish mobile number or pass through a browser-based authentication portal. Speeds vary depending on usage levels and location, with stronger signals in premium tourist districts.

Hotel And Accommodation Connectivity

Most hotels in Antalya, ranging from five-star resorts to boutique guesthouses, offer complimentary Wi-Fi access as a standard service. In higher-end establishments, the network extends across rooms, lobbies, poolsides, and conference centers, supporting video calls and media streaming with little interruption. However, in budget lodgings or older buildings, signal strength can fluctuate depending on your room's distance from the router. Some hotels restrict high-speed connectivity to premium guests, charging a nominal fee for extended bandwidth. It is advisable to inquire about network reliability and coverage upon check-in to ensure it aligns with one's digital needs during the stay.

Mobile Data And Local Sim Cards

For visitors who require constant internet access, purchasing a local Turkish SIM card is the most reliable solution. Major network providers in Antalya include Turkcell, Vodafone Turkey, and Türk Telekom, all of which offer competitive tourist packages that bundle data, calls, and texts. SIM cards can be purchased at Antalya Airport, shopping malls, or local telecom shops, with a valid passport required for registration. Coverage throughout Antalya is robust, extending well into suburban districts and even outlying natural parks. Mobile internet speeds are generally high, with 4.5G technology widely implemented and 5G rollout underway in select zones.

Internet Cafés And Co-Working Spaces

While the era of traditional internet cafés is declining, several such venues still operate in Antalya, particularly in central districts and student-heavy areas. These spots cater to gamers, digital workers, or those in need of printing and desktop access. More common now are co-working spaces, such as Workinton or Kolektif House, which attract remote professionals and digital nomads. These offer not just high-speed internet but also air-conditioned lounges, refreshments, and power-ready desks. Antalya's growing reputation as a digital nomad destination means these hubs are increasing in number and sophistication, providing a conducive environment for work and collaboration.

Internet Speed And National Infrastructure

Turkey's internet infrastructure has steadily improved in recent years, and Antalya benefits directly from this national progress. Average broadband speeds are adequate for streaming, conferencing, and uploading media, although occasional slowdowns can occur during peak evening hours. Fibre-optic connections are becoming more common in residential and commercial areas, particularly in newly developed suburbs. Antalya's telecommunications services are regulated and monitored, ensuring reasonable compliance with international standards. Though not yet on par with some Western European cities in terms of speed, Antalya's connectivity easily meets the expectations of modern travellers, students, and professionals visiting the city.

5.12 Visitor Centers and Tourist Assistance

Antalya offers a well-structured network of visitor centers and tourist help desks strategically placed across key entry points and high-traffic areas. These centers serve as the bridge between travelers and the city's endless offerings, ensuring that no visitor feels lost or unassisted. From first-time arrivals at the airport to seasoned explorers wandering through the historic Kaleiçi district, these services provide practical support, cultural insight, and real-time guidance that elevate the overall travel experience in Antalya.

Antalya Tourist Information Office – Kaleiçi District
At the heart of Antalya's old town, the Antalya Tourist Information Office in Kaleiçi serves as one of the most vital hubs for visitors seeking practical guidance and cultural insights. Located at Atatürk Caddesi No:42, this center is strategically positioned near Hadrian's Gate and is easily accessible by foot from many boutique hotels and historic attractions. The staff here are multilingual and equipped to provide maps, transportation advice, and up-to-date event listings, ensuring visitors get the most out of their experience. They offer tailored recommendations for nearby restaurants, beaches, and museums depending on visitors' interests and time constraints. The office is open daily, including weekends, and provides free brochures and heritage walking guides.

Antalya Airport Tourist Help Desk – Domestic and International Terminals
For those arriving by air, the tourist assistance counters at Antalya Airport's Terminals 1 and 2 act as the first welcoming point for international and domestic travelers. Located within the arrival halls, these desks are staffed by English-speaking personnel trained to assist with hotel bookings, airport transport options, and local customs procedures. The counters also supply free maps, updated flight and bus schedules, and emergency contact details, making it a critical starting point for new arrivals. They are particularly helpful during peak travel periods, providing instant assistance on delayed luggage, medical needs, and accommodation rerouting. The presence of these desks reinforces Antalya's commitment to seamless and safe visitor transitions.

Konyaaltı Beach Visitor Kiosk – Coastal Orientation and Services
Positioned along the popular Konyaaltı Beach promenade near the Aquarium junction, this coastal visitor kiosk is geared towards beachgoers and families exploring Antalya's seaside attractions. The small but resourceful booth provides tide updates, water safety information, and directions to amenities such as showers, restrooms, and dining options. Staff can help locate nearby parking spaces, advise on sunbed rentals, and recommend child-friendly zones along the beach. During summer, they coordinate with lifeguards and local police for enhanced visitor safety. It's an ideal stop for spontaneous planning, especially

for those unsure whether to stay by the shore or venture inland for cultural sightseeing.

Antalya Intercity Bus Terminal Visitor Point
The visitor center situated within the Antalya Intercity Bus Terminal (Otogar), at Kepez Mahallesi, caters primarily to travelers navigating regional routes across Turkey. It provides real-time updates on bus departures, ticketing guidance, and details on luggage storage and waiting area services. Staff here are skilled in helping international tourists with connections to Cappadocia, Pamukkale, or coastal towns like Kas and Alanya. Additionally, they offer assistance on public transport within Antalya, including tram and minibus networks. For budget-conscious travelers and backpackers, this center is an essential touchpoint for advice on navigating the country's extensive coach systems affordably and efficiently.

Lara Tourism Information Desk – East Antalya Hospitality Support
Located near the TerraCity Shopping Centre along Lara Caddesi, this tourist information desk caters to visitors staying in the city's luxurious eastern beachfront resorts. It is ideal for travelers requiring restaurant reservations, wellness center referrals, or private tour bookings in the Düden Waterfalls and Lower Lara area. The assistants also help guests in coordinating shuttle services, identifying cultural venues like Sandland, and managing lost-item reports. Their cooperation with local hotels ensures that travelers get timely updates on weather forecasts, VIP events, and safety alerts. It functions as both a convenience point and a cultural gateway, enriching the visitor experience through well-informed, prompt guidance.

CHAPTER 6
GASTRONOMIC DELIGHTS

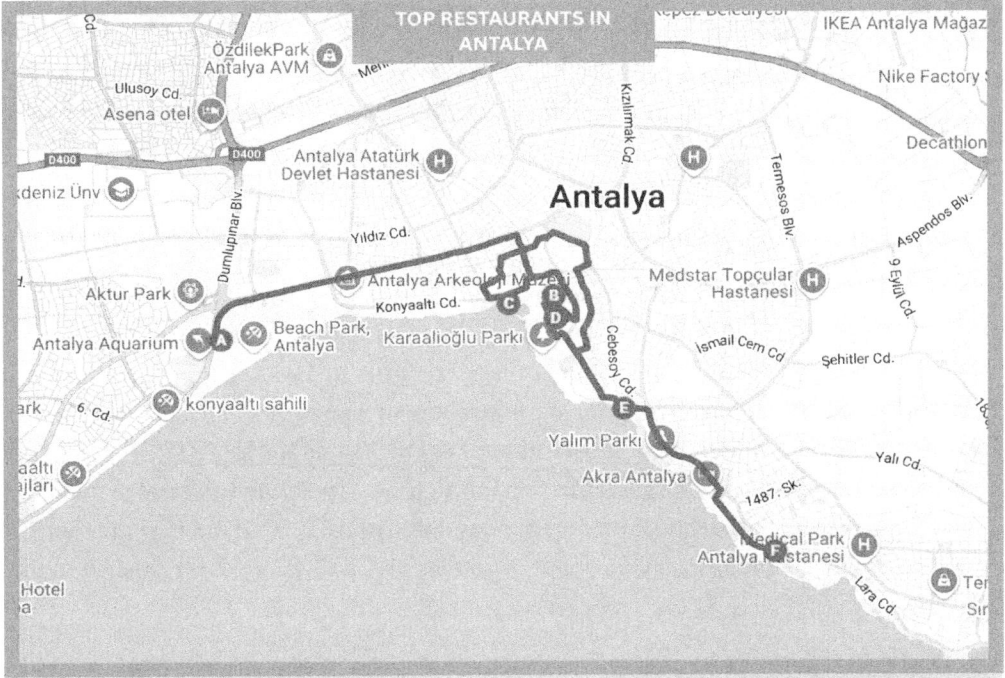

Directions from 7 Mehmet, Meltem, Muratpaşa/Antalya, Türkiye to Göz Balık Lara, Şirinyalı, Lara Caddesi, Muratpaşa/Antalya, Türkiye

A
7 Mehmet, Meltem, Muratpaşa/Antalya, Türkiye

B
Seraser Fine Dining Restaurant, Selçuk, Paşa Cami Sokak, Muratpaşa/Antalya, Türkiye

C
Arma Restaurant, Selçuk, Selçuk Mah, Muratpaşa/Antalya, Türkiye

D
Vanilla Restaurant, Barbaros, Hesapçı Sokak, Muratpaşa/Antalya, Türkiye

E
Lara Balık, Gençlik, Tevfik Işık Caddesi, Muratpaşa/Antalya, Türkiye

F
Göz Balık Lara, Şirinyalı, Lara Caddesi, Muratpaşa/Antalya, Türkiye

6.1 Dining Options and Top Restaurants

Antalya's culinary environment reflects a city deeply anchored in its heritage yet open to the evolving demands of global tastes. With the Mediterranean coast on one side and centuries of history behind it, the city's restaurant offerings provide more than just food—they deliver an experience shaped by tradition, geography, and a strong sense of hospitality. From long standing Turkish kitchens that follow age-old recipes to modern dining rooms reinterpreting Anatolian ingredients, each establishment offers something distinct.

7 Mehmet

Positioned along Dumlupınar Boulevard, just across from Atatürk Culture Park, 7 Mehmet is an enduring symbol of authentic Turkish cuisine in Antalya. The menu gives attention to regional classics—grilled meats, lamb slow-cooked in clay ovens, and a wide range of traditional appetizers, all accompanied by Turkish wines and local spirits like raki. The restaurant has built its reputation over decades, and its standards remain high both in service and in the quality of ingredients. Guests are welcomed every day from 10:30 in the morning until 11 at night. Bookings can be made through +90 242 238 52 00 or their online platform.

Seraser Fine Dining

Located inside the historic Kaleiçi district at Tuzcular Mahallesi, Seraser operates from a carefully restored stone mansion, bringing together Antalya's old-world charm and upscale culinary ambition. It specializes in creatively presented dishes such as braised lamb with sweet reductions, house-made pastas, and vegetarian courses that highlight seasonal produce. Lighting is understated and elegant, with interiors that respect the building's original design. The kitchen opens at noon and closes at 11 PM, while the restaurant stays open until midnight, ideal for those who appreciate long, relaxed meals. You can reach them for reservations at +90 242 247 60 15.

Arma Restaurant

Overlooking the old harbor at İskele Caddesi No:75, Arma Restaurant combines heritage architecture with a setting that frames Antalya's marina perfectly. With a menu heavy on seafood, diners can enjoy grilled fish, octopus, and pasta inspired by Mediterranean flavors, all served on a terrace that remains open throughout the year. The restaurant's location once served industrial purposes in the 19th century, now repurposed for elegant waterfront dining. Open daily from

11 AM until 11 PM, it is strongly advised to book ahead by calling +90 242 244 97 10 due to its popularity with both locals and visitors.

Vanilla Restaurant

Vanilla sits quietly along Hesapçı Sokak in Kaleiçi, offering a contemporary and minimalistic approach to Turkish and international dining. The kitchen turns out flavorful dishes such as marinated meats, regional vegetarian specialties, and creatively plated starters, all paired with local wines or cold draft beer. The ambiance is relaxed, with understated décor and a focus on letting the food speak for itself. It remains open from midday until around 10:15 in the evening, with daily service. For specific dietary inquiries or reservations, the team is available on +90 242 247 60 13.

Lara Balık

Set on Tevfik Işık Caddesi No:8, in the Gençlik Mahallesi area, Lara Balık places emphasis on fresh, locally caught seafood and simple yet precise execution. The dishes here range from fire-grilled fish to plates of appetizers seasoned with olive oil, lemon, and Mediterranean herbs. Guests enjoy both indoor and outdoor dining, with the open-air section offering partial views of the sea. Open every day from 9 in the morning until midnight, this restaurant is ideal for everything from lunch to late-night dining. To avoid waiting times, guests can reserve via +90 242 313 13 99.

Göz Balık Lara

Positioned along Lara Caddesi No:113/A in the Şirinyalı neighborhood, Göz Balık Lara serves dishes that fuse local seafood with subtle international influences. Its linguine in tomato-garlic sauce, grilled shrimp, and stuffed mussels are standout favorites, accompanied by crisp white wines sourced from Turkish vineyards. With high ceilings and wide tables, it comfortably handles both intimate dinners and group celebrations. The restaurant welcomes diners from noon until nearly midnight daily. To ensure availability, you may call ahead at +90 543 529 99 86.

6.2 Local Cuisine and Specialties (Doner Kebab, Baklava)

Antalya is more than just a coastal paradise of turquoise waters and Roman ruins. Its culinary heritage is a living, breathing extension of its Anatolian heart, where spices, techniques, and recipes are passed from generation to generation. For visitors, diving into the local cuisine is not a side experience—it is the experience. From sizzling meats carved straight from vertical spits to sticky desserts layered with history, the food in Antalya speaks of its deep cultural layers, Mediterranean roots, and timeless Turkish hospitality.

Doner Kebab

Doner kebab is perhaps the most visible emblem of Turkish street food, and in Antalya, it is found on every corner, rotating slowly on vertical spits. Local establishments such as Şişçi Ramazan and Tırnakçıoğlu Döner on Güllük Street prepare their doner using seasoned lamb or chicken layered with thin fat slices for richness. Expect to pay around 80 to 120 TL depending on portion size and whether it's served in pita, wrap, or on a plate with rice. It's best eaten fresh off the spit, and locals usually pair it with ayran, a cold yogurt-based drink that balances the meat's intensity. Tourists are advised to look for places where locals queue, as freshness and turnover matter most.

Baklava

Baklava in Antalya is an art form, crafted layer by layer with precision. You'll find the best examples at Sultanoğlu Baklava near MarkAntalya Mall or at the revered Baklavacı Güllüoğlu, an offshoot of the Gaziantep original. Visitors should try to eat it freshly made, ideally within hours of baking, and always with Turkish tea or bitter Turkish coffee for contrast. Keep in mind that pistachio-based baklava is more traditional in Antalya than walnut varieties.

Piyaz

A humble-looking yet rich bean salad, piyaz in Antalya is unlike that served in other parts of Turkey. Here, it's elevated with a generous drizzle of tahini, garlic, lemon juice, and olive oil, turning it into a creamy, protein-rich side dish or light main course. Try it at Piyazcı Ahmet in Muratpaşa, where a plate goes for about 60 TL. This local specialty often accompanies grilled köfte and is enjoyed at midday when the sun's heat calls for something refreshing but substantial. Tourists should ensure they ask for "Antalya usulü piyaz" to get the tahini-based regional version.

Kabak Tatlısı

This seemingly simple dessert—pumpkin cooked in sugar syrup—is a traditional Antalya treat, often topped with crushed walnuts or tahini. The pumpkin is slow-cooked until tender and translucent, creating a naturally sweet and subtly earthy flavour. Best places to try this are at Arma Restaurant overlooking the marina or at 7 Mehmet, where a serving is about 70 TL. Locals typically eat it during winter, though it's available year-round in tourist-frequented spots. Visitors should pair it with unsweetened tea or mineral water to offset the syrupy texture.

Gözleme

Gözleme is the go-to traditional flatbread snack in Antalya, filled with choices ranging from spinach and cheese to minced meat and potato, and cooked on a convex griddle known as a saç. Village-style gözleme can be found in the old town (Kaleiçi) or in roadside stalls along Lara Road. Prices vary between 40 to 70 TL depending on filling. Tourists will find this is often made fresh on the spot by women in traditional attire, and it's best eaten hot with homemade ayran. Unlike fast food, this dish retains its rustic, homemade roots and is perfect for a quick yet authentic bite.

6.3 Food Tours and Culinary Experiences

Exploring Antalya's food scene takes visitors on gastronomic journeys which is not merely about what is eaten, but how and where it is prepared and shared. From guided street food walks through bustling quarters to hands-on sessions in professional kitchens, each experience is an entry point into the local soul.

Antalya Local Food Tour by Excursion Market

Departing daily from 2000 Plaza near Hadrian's Gate, this guided food tour runs from 11:30 in the morning until approximately 14:30 in the afternoon. Over three hours, participants follow a route that includes multiple eateries renowned for their authentic Turkish dishes, including kebabs, mezes and sweets. English-speaking guides explain each dish's background, while optional add-ons like Turkish coffee or fresh juices enhance the tour. Booking is done online through Excursion Market, with a partial prepayment and the rest settled on the day of the tour. Guests walk between locations, making it essential to wear comfortable shoes and come prepared for a slow, flavour-filled stroll.

Private Antalya Street Food Tour

This customised street food tour is arranged directly through local tour operators and offers private pick-up and drop-off at the visitor's accommodation. There is no fixed start time, making it ideal for those who prefer flexibility in scheduling. Guests are guided through open-air markets, small food kiosks and lesser-known street corners, tasting regional snacks like börek, tantuni and stuffed mussels. A private driver and an English-speaking guide accompany the group, which typically consists of four people or fewer. Though transportation and guidance are covered, food costs are paid individually at each stop. This format suits travellers looking to blend culinary discovery with a relaxed, personalised pace.

Culinary Walking Tour with Yeliz Y

This walking-based food experience, hosted by local expert Yeliz Y, focuses on Antalya's quieter alleys and traditional neighbourhoods. Operating year-round and only by advance booking, it begins at a mutually decided meeting point and lasts about five hours. The tour introduces small groups to traditional pastry shops, tea gardens, old-style taverns and local markets. Food, including both savoury and sweet samples, is included in the total price. Private transport is available if needed between more distant stops, and the guide tailors the route based on guest interests. Prices are calculated per group with additional charges for extra participants, and full payment is made online prior to the tour.

Ananas Cooking School Antalya

Located at 1533 Sokak No. 27/A in Şirinyalı Mahallesi, this school specialises in hands-on culinary classes and runs sessions daily upon prior arrangement. Led by Chef Ekaterina, each class covers the preparation and plating of traditional or international cuisine, such as Turkish, French or Japanese. Classes usually run two to three hours and end with a shared meal and the chance to take recipes home. Bookings are handled online, and costs vary depending on the type of cuisine and group size. All tools and ingredients are supplied, and the school maintains a professional kitchen environment. Group sizes are kept small to allow personal guidance and deeper engagement.

Saturday Market Food Tasting Experience

The Saturday food market, held weekly at Laura Market area in Şirinyalı (1500 Sk. No. 10 A), is a local gathering space known for both its fresh ingredients and ready-to-eat items. Open from 09:30 until early evening, visitors can sample items such as gözleme, grilled corn and handmade sweets directly from the producers. The market also offers cheese, olives, herbs and fruit that can be tasted on the spot or packed to go. No reservation is required, and visitors pay individually for whatever they choose to try. The open layout encourages exploration at your own pace, while locals are usually open to discussing their products and offering cooking tips.

Lara Grand Bazaar Food Experience

Situated at Lara Turizm Yolu No. 69 in Kemerağzı, this expansive market operates every day from early morning until midnight. While shopping for textiles and souvenirs draws many, the food offerings are equally notable. Dozens of kiosks and food stands line the complex, serving a wide range of meals and snacks from kebabs to flatbreads and freshly made sweets. Seating areas allow for relaxed dining within the bazaar complex, and some vendors offer combo meals for a fixed price. No booking is needed, and visitors can sample freely, buying as much or as little as they prefer. This spot offers a relaxed and informal way to enjoy authentic Turkish street food while absorbing the commercial pulse of Antalya.

6.4 Local Markets and Food Shops

Antalya's dynamic food culture owes much to its enduring tradition of open markets and specialty food shops where locals and visitors interact over the freshest produce, seafood, and regional staples. Beyond the glimmer of beach resorts and modern malls, the heart of the city beats strongest where ingredients are still selected by hand, prices can be negotiated, and recipes are passed along with each purchase. These markets and shops are not only places of commerce, but also living spaces where the memory of Ottoman dishes and Mediterranean customs remains part of the daily routine.

Çarşamba Pazarı

Set along Atatürk Boulevard in Pınarbaşı Mahallesi every Wednesday, Çarşamba Pazarı becomes a vibrant forum where local farmers offer their harvest and vendors deal in everything from spices to cheese. Fresh produce like tomatoes and cucumbers is sold between eight and fifteen lira per kilo, while olive oil and regional cheese cost between sixty and seventy lira. Most vendors accept cash, and while some have card readers, bringing small change makes for quicker transactions. Early morning visits yield the best selection and a cooler shopping experience before midday temperatures rise. Shoppers should carry their own bags and be ready for fast-paced exchanges and occasional tastings.

Aşağı Pazar

Located in Kültür Mahallesi, Aşağı Pazar offers a traditional market setting where foods, textiles, and handmade products share space in long rows of stalls. Preserved goods like honey and jam are often priced from forty to eighty lira, while woven fabrics and scarves go for fifty to a hundred lira depending on quality. Visitors often find this market best explored in the afternoon when the crowd thins slightly and stallholders are more open to conversation. The atmosphere is informal but deeply rooted in local habits that date back generations.

Antalya Balık Pazarı

At İsmet Paşa Caddesi near the harbour, Antalya's fish market draws early risers in search of the freshest catch brought in overnight from the surrounding waters. Fish like sea bass and mackerel sell for between eighty and one hundred lira per kilo, while prawns fetch slightly more at up to one hundred and twenty lira. Buyers are encouraged to inspect the eyes and scales of the fish before purchase to ensure quality. On-site eateries will grill your fish for around thirty lira, offering a quick and authentic seafood meal. Visiting before eight in the morning offers the best access to both variety and value.

5M Migros Grand Plaza

In the Döşemealtı area, the 5M Migros branch inside Grand Plaza Shopping Centre serves as a clean, well-organised alternative to street markets, catering to both everyday needs and specialty food interests. Shoppers can find olives at sixty lira per kilo, imported cheese at one hundred and twenty, and fresh produce sold by box for fifty to seventy lira. This store is known for frequent promotions tied to its digital loyalty scheme, and receipts are sent via app for convenience. With air conditioning, wide aisles, and clearly marked shelves, the environment supports calm shopping away from street-level activity.

MarkAntalya Food Market

Turkish delight starts at twenty lira per hundred grams, while jars of local olives and preserves sell for around fifty to eighty lira. Staff are trained to guide first-time visitors, providing samples and sharing preparation tips for unfamiliar items. The experience is curated but still authentic, retaining Antalya's flavour even within a commercial setting. Best times to visit are mid-day, when all shops are open and foot traffic allows for leisurely browsing.

Tarihi Piyazcı Aziz

On Toklu Sokak No:1 in the historic Kaleiçi quarter, Tarihi Piyazcı Aziz continues serving its namesake dish with a recipe that dates back decades. A hearty plate of piyaz—a white bean salad enriched with tahini and vinegar—is offered at fifteen lira, with add-ons like egg or extra onions priced modestly. The small dining space fills up quickly by midday, so early arrival ensures a seat and faster service. This humble eatery only accepts cash and operates on fast turnover, where regulars and newcomers alike share bench seating and conversation. The surrounding lanes make a charming follow-up walk after your meal.

CHAPTER 7
DAY TRIPS AND EXCURSIONS

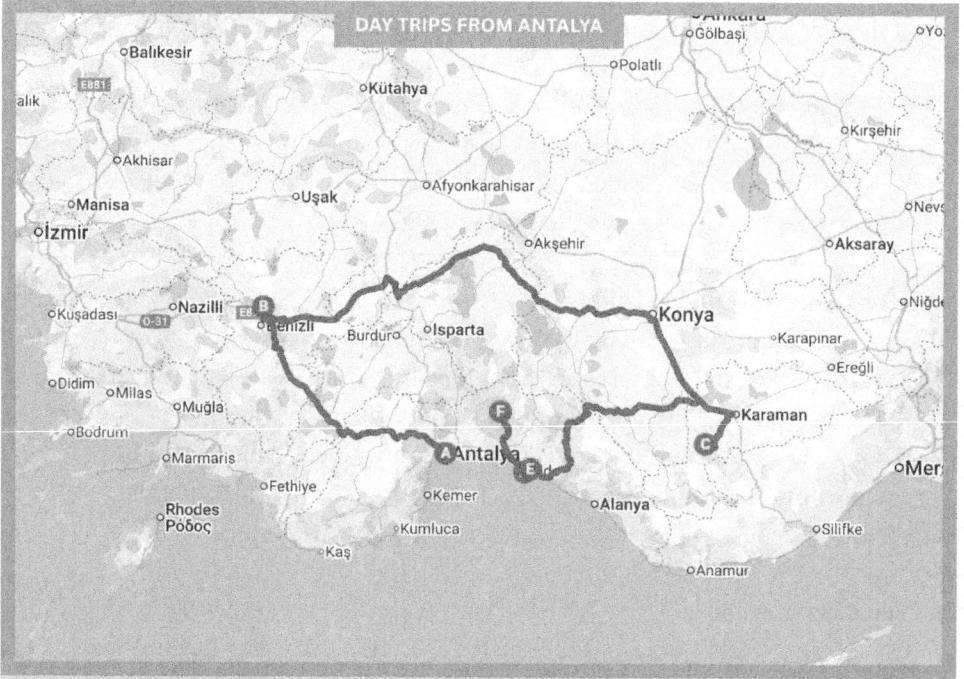

Directions from Antalya, Türkiye to Köprülü Canyon National Park, Bozyaka, Manavgat/Antalya, Türkiye

A
Antalya,
Türkiye

B
Hierapolis, Pamukkale,
Denizli, Türkiye

C
Taurus Mountains, Çatak/Karaman
Center/Karaman, Türkiye

D
Side Ancient City, Selimiye Neighborhood,
Çağla Street, Manavgat/Antalya, Türkiye

E
Manavgat,
Antalya, Türkiye

F
Köprülü Canyon National Park, Bozyaka,
Manavgat/Antalya, Türkiye

7.1 Pamukkale and Hierapolis

For anyone staying in Antalya and craving a day of wonder that is rooted both in natural phenomena and ancient civilization, a trip to Pamukkale and Hierapolis offers an unforgettable experience. These twin sites, located in the Denizli Province of southwestern Turkey, form one of the most iconic attractions in the country. From the gleaming white thermal terraces to the timeworn remnants of Roman history, the journey from Antalya to Pamukkale takes approximately three and a half hours by car, but the reward far outweighs the drive.

Walking Through the Travertine Terraces

One of the first activities that captivates visitors is walking barefoot along the famed travertine terraces of Pamukkale. These calcified formations were created by the mineral-laden thermal waters that continue to trickle down the slope today, solidifying into hardened steps of gleaming white. With temperatures varying across different pools, the warm water combined with the surreal setting creates a sensory experience that is both relaxing and arresting. It is mandatory to remove shoes to protect the delicate deposits, and visitors often pause for long moments to soak their feet while gazing at the horizon of the valley below. This activity isn't simply about sightseeing—it's a visceral encounter with nature's ability to sculpt beauty over millennia.

Swimming in Cleopatra's Antique Pool

Cleopatra's Pool is a historic geothermal spring reputedly enjoyed by the Egyptian queen herself during the Roman era. Today, the water remains naturally heated, averaging around 36°C, and is filled with ancient marble columns that fell during an earthquake and now lie submerged, adding to the experience. Swimming here is unlike any typical spa visit—it feels like gliding through history. Visitors pay a separate fee to enter the pool, and lockers and changing rooms are available on-site. For those who want to linger, the nearby café offers light meals and refreshments in the shade, allowing time to relax before or after the swim.

Exploring the Ruins of Hierapolis

Beyond the thermal pools lies Hierapolis, an ancient Greco-Roman city built in the 2nd century BCE, now a UNESCO World Heritage Site. The expansive ruins stretch over a plateau and include a Byzantine church, temples, Roman baths, and an extensive necropolis. Walking through Hierapolis gives a strong sense of how urban life functioned at the frontier between culture and geography. Stone columns, some broken and others defiant against time, line the old colonnaded streets while the silence of the site, punctuated by birds and the crunch of gravel underfoot, allows a kind of reflective solitude. With each step, visitors uncover new dimensions of a city that once flourished in tandem with the healing reputation of its thermal springs.

Sitting Inside the Ancient Theatre

Carved into the hillside and still largely intact, the ancient theatre of Hierapolis is one of the highlights of any visit. It held up to 15,000 spectators in its prime and today stands as a silent colossus of Roman architectural mastery. From the top rows, the view stretches over the valley below and across to the travertine terraces, reinforcing how this city was built to harmonize with its environment. Climbing up the stone seating, one can imagine the dramatic performances, political announcements, and public ceremonies that once animated the space. The atmosphere here is not recreated or commercialised—it is preserved in its raw and commanding form, allowing imagination to do the rest.

Wandering the Necropolis and Thermal Baths

The necropolis contains over a thousand tombs, from modest sarcophagi to elaborate mausoleums, scattered across a rocky plain. These burial structures speak volumes about the status, beliefs, and customs of those who once lived here. Some were constructed for local elites, while others were intended for visitors who sought healing from the thermal springs but never left. Just beyond the necropolis are the ruins of Roman thermal baths that were once integral to the town's function as a healing center. Standing among these remnants, it becomes clear how deeply intertwined wellness, death, and community were in the ancient world.

Travel Practicalities and Additional Tips
The best way to reach Pamukkale from Antalya is by hiring a private vehicle or joining a full-day guided tour, many of which include pick-up and return transport, entrance fees, and a lunch stop. Tours typically depart early in the morning and return by evening, with routes passing through the scenic Taurus Mountains and rural landscapes. Entrance to the site currently costs around 700 Turkish Lira, with extra fees for Cleopatra's Pool. Summer months can be hot, so visitors should wear breathable clothing, carry bottled water, and use sun protection. Although it's possible to visit independently, guided tours offer historical insights that deepen the experience and ensure access to all key areas without logistical hassle.

7.2 Kemer and the Taurus Mountains

Taurus Mountains strike a stark contrast to Antalya's city rhythms, trading bustling streets for mountain ridges and raw Mediterranean beauty. Travelling just beyond the city's borders, visitors encounter a different face of southern Turkey, one where forested hills roll into the sea and ancient ruins lie scattered in remote valleys. The road to Kemer curves through terrain that grows steadily greener and more dramatic, culminating in a backdrop of pine-studded mountains and azure sea.

Exploring Phaselis Ancient City by the Sea

Among the most compelling activities near Kemer is a visit to the ruins of Phaselis, an ancient Lycian city located where the mountains meet the coast. The site lies roughly 16 kilometres south of Kemer and can be reached by car, taxi, or group tour departing from Antalya. Visitors walk through the remnants of aqueducts, Roman baths, and an agora that once served merchants trading goods between Greece, Egypt, and Asia Minor. A short path leads directly to the seafront, where calm waters lap at what remains of a harbour that once welcomed fleets. The mix of archaeological intrigue and seclusion by the shore offers a rich historical retreat away from crowds.

Riding the Olympos Teleferik to Mount Tahtalı Summit

Another highlight is the cable car ride up Mount Tahtalı, often referred to by its ancient name, Olympos. Located about 15 kilometres from Kemer, this experience begins at the base station near Tekirova and climbs over 2,300 metres to a peak that offers commanding views of the Mediterranean and Taurus range. The 10-minute ascent is an experience in itself, rising above forests, clouds, and rocky slopes that seem to fold endlessly toward the horizon. At the summit, visitors often find snow in spring and autumn, a surreal contrast to the beaches far below. The mountaintop terrace has a café and plenty of open space to breathe in the clean, alpine air.

Whitewater Rafting in the Köprülü Canyon National Park

For those inclined toward physical thrill, whitewater rafting through Köprülü Canyon offers a full-day adventure unlike anything else around Antalya. Though slightly inland, the canyon lies within driving reach and is often offered as part of a group excursion with transport, gear, and lunch included. The river winds through a gorge flanked by pine forests and limestone cliffs, and depending on the season, the rapids vary from gentle to moderately intense. Rafting crews are usually accompanied by professional guides, and the excursion includes stops at ancient bridges, swimming holes, and scenic overlooks. It is a raw and physical way to engage with the Taurus Mountains' elemental strength.

Off-Road Jeep Safari Through the Taurus Highlands

The jeep safaris that snake through the dirt roads of the Taurus Mountains give travellers a chance to witness life in Turkey's rural highlands. These tours often begin from Kemer or Göynük and take a rugged course past small villages, citrus groves, and streams tumbling through the rock. The air gets cooler as the elevation climbs, and drivers make regular stops for panoramic views and interaction with locals. These outings frequently include lunch at a mountainside eatery, where grilled trout or lamb stew is served with fresh bread and tea. It's a rough but rewarding ride into landscapes that still live by the seasons rather than the clock.

Swimming and Sunbathing at Moonlight Beach

For a more laid-back excursion, Moonlight Beach in Kemer is an inviting stretch of sand with clear waters and a peaceful vibe that contrasts sharply with Antalya's busier shores. Just a short walk from Kemer's marina, the beach is accessible by minibus or taxi from the city, and many tours include time here. The beach is lined with cafes and loungers, and the shallow waters make it ideal for swimming or paddle boating. As the sun drops behind the jagged Taurus peaks, the beach takes on a calm, almost cinematic quality, drawing both locals and travellers into a slower rhythm that marks the end of a day well spent.

Reaching Kemer and the Mountain Region from Antalya

Getting from Antalya to Kemer and the surrounding Taurus Mountains is straightforward and takes under an hour by road. Buses run regularly from Antalya's main Otogar to Kemer, or visitors can rent cars for more flexibility, particularly if the journey includes off-road segments or lesser-known valleys. Organised excursions often pick guests up from their hotels, offering guided itineraries with meals, transfers, and entrance fees bundled into one. The drive itself becomes part of the experience, passing through tunnels, alongside cliffs, and over riverbeds that signal the region's wild character.

7.3 Side Ancient City

Spending a day in Side, one of Turkey's most enduringly evocative archaeological sites, is not just a tour through crumbling ruins, but a step back into a world shaped by ancient ambition and maritime trade. Located along the Mediterranean coastline, around eighty kilometres east of Antalya, Side was once a thriving Greco-Roman port city. Today it draws visitors with its remarkable ruins and a lively atmosphere that hums with the distant echoes of a time long gone.

Exploring the Roman Theatre and its Timeless Grandeur

The Roman Theatre in Side is the city's most commanding presence, a semi-circular marvel that once held up to fifteen thousand spectators. Towering arches and a multi-tiered cavea form the spine of this structure, giving visitors a sense of the grand scale Roman entertainment once occupied. Walking through its stone aisles, you'll sense the weight of silence where actors once performed and gladiators stood at the mercy of roars. Its design blends Greek and Roman techniques, evident in the freestanding structure and the scaenae frons that rises like a backdrop to forgotten performances. Photographs don't do justice to the atmosphere; only by standing in its centre does one fully comprehend the Roman appetite for drama and spectacle.

Walking the Colonnaded Street and Imagining Ancient Commerce

Stretching through the centre of the archaeological zone, the Colonnaded Street was once Side's commercial backbone, its marble paving still revealing grooves worn by ancient cart wheels. Lined by fragmented columns and broken capitals, the avenue showcases how life once flowed through the city in organised chaos, with traders, buyers, and political figures brushing shoulders. At its heart lies a nymphaeum, once a decorative fountain that drew water from aqueducts and supplied it to nearby baths and homes. Exploring this street is not just about looking—it is about placing oneself in the footsteps of history, hearing in your mind the bargaining voices and rhythmic footfall of a city at its zenith. The scent of sea air mixes with the dry perfume of ancient stone, intensifying the time-travel effect.

Visiting the Temple of Apollo at Sunset

No visit to Side is complete without standing before the Temple of Apollo, its white columns reaching into the sky as the sun prepares to slip beneath the Mediterranean. The temple stands on the edge of the ancient harbour, and its enduring pillars have become a symbol of Side's identity. Dedicated to the god of light and music, this site offers not just aesthetic value but spiritual depth. The golden hour draws both photographers and reflective travellers who stand silently, watching the interplay of light on fluted stone. Some of the capitals and fragments of the temple remain scattered, whispering of what once was a full structure that crowned the city's devotion to divine order and cultural sophistication. Time seems to pause here, allowing thoughts to linger a little longer.

Discovering the Side Museum and Its Unearthed Treasures

Housed in what was once a Roman bath complex, the Side Museum offers a carefully curated glimpse into the artifacts and art recovered from the surrounding area. The collection includes intricately carved sarcophagi, Roman statues, and Hellenistic altars, each piece a remnant of a complex society built on trade, conquest, and religious devotion. While the ruins outside tell the story of architecture and space, the museum pieces offer intimate insights into personal life—jewellery, tools, and inscribed stones that reveal names, professions, and dedications. Walking through the chambers, cooled by thick stone walls, is a quiet experience that brings balance to the grandeur of the open-air ruins. It reminds visitors that beneath every monumental column was a human story, deeply felt and now preserved.

Wandering the Ancient Harbour and Enjoying the Present

Side's ancient harbour, once vital for the city's economic power, is today a place where antiquity meets leisure. With the sea lapping gently against stone quays and yachts now bobbing where Roman merchant ships once docked, it offers a moment of relaxation with a historical backdrop. The surrounding area is alive with cafés and small restaurants, where the scent of grilled fish competes with salty breezes. Walking along the promenade, one can view submerged ruins beneath the clear water, ghost-like outlines of structures that once supported the maritime life of the city. This is the ideal spot to end a day trip, allowing the eyes to rest while the mind processes the weight of what has been seen. Time in Side doesn't just pass; it folds and mingles with the present.

7.4 Manavgat and the Köprülü Canyon

A journey from Antalya into the heart of the province reveals a landscape shaped by flowing water, age-worn stone, and quiet villages that remain untouched by modern bustle. As the road winds away from the coast, the air cools and the scenery shifts from sun-baked roads to forested slopes and dramatic river gorges. This expedition blends moments of adrenaline with chances to pause beside ancient bridges or sip tea by gentle rapids..

Cruising the Manavgat River and Visiting the Falls

A boat glides silently beneath leafy overhangs as fishermen cast lines from the shallows, their patience mirrored in the gentle current. The wide, low cascade of the Manavgat Falls spills into a placid pool, inviting relaxed observation rather than frantic photography. Wooden decks and riverside cafés provide spots to linger, where locals share stories over steaming glasses of apple tea. Dragonflies alight on reeds while the water reflects shifting cloud patterns above. A final stretch carries the vessel into a marshy delta, merging fresh and salt water in a scene that beckons swimmers.

Ascending to the Ruins of Ancient Selge

High above the canyon floor, Selge's silent stones stand testament to Roman ambition and Pisidian resilience. A narrow drive climbs through pine-clad slopes, leaving modern life behind with each hairpin turn. The seating of the old amphitheatre still commands views across the valley, its worn tiers whispering of long-ago performances. Columns lean and capitals lie scattered, tangled in wild grasses where goats now graze unbothered. Standing on those weathered steps, one senses the ebb of history echoing through the mountain air.

Rafting the Whitewater of Köprülü Canyon

Adrenaline surges as rafts plunge into foaming rapids, guided by seasoned instructors who pair local knowledge with safety routines. Cold, crystalline water carves its way between towering cliffs, the spray invigorating on a warm afternoon. Every rapid offers a new challenge, from gentle chutes that tease beginners to roaring torrents that thrill veterans. Midway through the descent, the raft slows near a shaded bank, where swimmers can plunge in or simply drift beneath overhanging pines. By journey's end, laughter mingles with the echo of rushing water, and a hearty riverside meal awaits.

Crossing the Ancient Oluk Bridge

Stepping onto the single-arch span built centuries ago feels like walking back through time, each stone laid by hands long vanished. Below, the river rushes through a constricted gorge, its volume amplified by the narrow channel. The bridge's gentle curve and rough-hewn blocks speak of engineering that outlasts fleeting fashions. Silence reigns apart from the water's roar and the soft whisper of wind brushing canyon walls. Pausing at its midpoint, visitors absorb the drama of height, depth, and the enduring craft of Roman builders.

Immersing in Manavgat's Market and Riverside Cuisine

Thursdays and Mondays bring the town alive with stalls laden with bright peppers, olives cured in brine, and fragrant spices piled high. Tea-sellers offer mint-infused warmth under canvas shades, where locals haggle and laugh with neighbours. After exploring every alley, the aroma of grilled river trout beckons from open-air restaurants lining the water's edge. Platters of stuffed grape leaves and bowls of tangy lentil soup accompany freshly baked flatbreads, all best savoured in languid conversation. As the afternoon light softens, the market's rhythm slows to match the gentle flow of the river.

Travel Practicalities and Recommendations

The journey from Antalya spans about seventy-five kilometres eastward, typically covered in ninety minutes by private car or organised tour. From Manavgat, a further forty-minute drive on winding, narrow roads leads into the heart of Köprülü Canyon National Park. Comfortable walking shoes are essential for uneven terrain, and sun protection remains critical even in shaded sections of the gorge. Booking rafting trips and guided ruin visits in advance ensures availability during peak summer months. Carrying water, snacks, and a lightweight rain jacket can make the excursion adaptable to changing weather and varying activity levels.

7.5 Boat Tours and Water Activities

Embarking on a maritime journey from Antalya offers an invitation to explore ancient ruins, hidden coves, and crystalline waters that have captivated seafarers for millennia. These excursions blend time-honored traditions of Turkish gulets and modern speedboats, ensuring every traveler finds their perfect aquatic adventure. Prepare to depart with essential gear, local tips, and fee details at your fingertips, ready for a day drenched in history and natural wonder.

Gulet Cruise to Phaselis and Yardımlı Bay

A traditional wooden gulet sets sail from Antalya's Old Harbour, navigating southeast to the ancient city of Phaselis perched on rocky inlets. The voyage is best undertaken between May and October when Mediterranean breezes are warm and seas calm. Visitors should bring sun protection, swimwear, and light snacks; a modest harbour fee of around 50 TRY per person covers mooring. On arrival, guests can step ashore to wander Roman ruins and marvel at centuries-old aqueducts before diving into Yardımlı Bay's translucent waters.

The gently rocking vessel, scented with cedar and salt, invites you to recline on plush cushions as history slips by.

Düden Waterfalls Boat Excursion

Departing eastward along the coastline, this boat tour sails past rugged cliffs to the point where Düden River dramatically plunges into the sea. Autumn through spring offers the most spectacular waterfall flow, though summer mornings still deliver a refreshing mist. Essentials include waterproof camera cases, a light jacket for spray, and a nominal ticket fee of roughly 30 TRY payable dockside. As the cascade thunders overhead, onlookers are treated to prismatic rainbows dancing on sea spray and the thunderous echo of falling water. The return leg follows a shoreline dotted with hidden grottoes, each begging for further exploration by kayak or snorkel.

High-Speed Powerboat to St. Nicholas Island

A high-speed powerboat slices through glittering waves towards the tiny isle associated with Saint Nicholas, lying just offshore of Demre. Optimal conditions fall between late spring and early autumn when winds are light and the sea mirror-smooth. Participants need sturdy shoes for rocky landings, bottled water, and the embarkation fee of approximately 100 TRY, which includes guiding service. Stepping onto the island, travelers encounter a Byzantine church and tombs carved into the cliffs, stark against the vivid blue horizon. The return journey thrills with spray-drenched speed and panoramic vistas of the Taurus Mountains rising from the shoreline.

Glass-Bottom Boat Voyage in Konyaaltı

Launching from Konyaaltı Beach, this glassbottom cruise reveals the underwater world without getting wet, cruising over reefs and seagrass meadows teeming with marine life. Late spring through early autumn provides the clearest visibility, ensuring you glimpse every darting fish and olive-coloured sea cucumber. Sunscreen, hats, and sunglasses are essential; a small boarding fee near 40 TRY grants access and guided marine commentary. Beneath the vessel's transparent hull, schools of colorful damselfish shimmer amid ancient amphora fragments scattered on the seabed. The gentle rocking of the boat and the cool shade of its canopy make for a tranquil aquatic safari.

Blue Cave Kayak Expedition

A short boat transfer from Antalya deposits adventurers at the entrance of a cobalt-blue sea cave, where lightweight kayaks await for a self-guided paddle inside. The best months run June through September when sunlight penetrates deep into the cavern, illuminating its walls in cerulean brilliance. Visitors must bring waterproof bags for cameras, life jackets supplied by operators, and a small park entrance charge of 25 TRY. Paddling through the low-arching tunnel, you emerge into a hidden lagoon that glows with refracted light and echoes of dripping stalactites. Every stroke through these hallowed waters offers a contemplative glimpse into nature's sculpted artistry.

Sea Trek Underwater Walking at Lara Beach

At Lara Beach, modern helmets allow you to breathe and stroll along the sandy seabed, surrounded by swaying sea grass and curious fish. Morning sessions from May to October avoid afternoon choppiness and deliver the best underwater clarity. Swimmers require comfortable swimwear, avoid loose jewelry, and pay a standard participation fee of around 150 TRY, which includes equipment and instruction. Descending five meters below the surface, the world above becomes a silvery ceiling as you encounter parrot fish nibbling at rocks and graceful rays gliding by. Emerging back on deck, participants receive water and fresh towels before returning to the sun-kissed shoreline.

CHAPTER 8
EVENTS AND FESTIVALS

8.1 Antalya Festival

Antalya, a coastal gem on Turkey's southern shores, is not only famed for its sunlit beaches and ancient ruins but also for its deeply rooted cultural festivities that unfold throughout the year. These events offer an immersive glimpse into the city's soul, merging history, artistry, and the spirited rhythm of Mediterranean life. Attending the Antalya Festival is not just about witnessing a celebration—it is about becoming part of something timeless, vibrant, and profoundly Turkish.

Antalya Golden Orange Film Festival

Held every October, the Antalya Golden Orange Film Festival is Turkey's most prestigious cinematic event and has been showcasing both domestic and international films since 1963. It takes place primarily at the Antalya Culture Center (Antalya Kültür Merkezi), located in the city centre, and is easily accessible by tram, bus, or taxi from any part of Antalya. Entry prices vary depending on the screening but are generally modest, making it accessible for all film enthusiasts. The festival is a powerful platform that honours Turkish cinema, while also drawing global talent, critics, and cinephiles into Antalya's creative orbit. Attendees can engage in film screenings, Q&A sessions with directors, open-air premieres, and workshops, which transform the city into a buzzing cinematic hub for a full week.

Antalya International Folk Music and Dance Festival
This annual event, typically held in September, brings together traditional dance troupes and folk music performers from across Turkey and around the world. Known locally as "Uluslararası Antalya Halk Dansları Festivali," it is primarily staged at open-air venues such as the ancient Aspendos Theatre and public squares across Antalya. Visitors can reach these sites by organised shuttle buses or regular public transport. The festival has no entry fee for street performances, though some theatre-based events may require a ticket. What makes it truly unique is the cultural exchange that takes place, as dancers in full traditional regalia perform regional routines that have been passed down through generations. It is more than a spectacle—it's a celebration of human heritage and a rare opportunity to witness Turkey's folk roots flourish in a modern setting.

Aspendos International Opera and Ballet Festival
This classical arts festival is staged every June within the breathtaking ruins of the 2,000-year-old Roman-built Aspendos Theatre, located just outside Antalya in the town of Serik. Reaching the site involves a one-hour drive from central Antalya, easily navigated via rental car, tour bus, or a well-connected dolmuş service. Ticket prices vary by performance and seating, but even the least expensive seat offers a world-class view beneath the open sky. The event holds deep national significance, marrying Turkey's reverence for the arts with one of its most iconic ancient landmarks. Audiences experience grand operas and ballets under the stars, surrounded by stone walls that once echoed the voices of Roman performers—an atmosphere so ethereal it leaves an indelible imprint on all who attend.

Antalya Sand Sculpture Festival
Commonly known by locals as "Sandland," this festival occurs annually from May through November along Lara Beach, transforming tonnes of sand into monumental works of art. Located in the eastern district of Lara, it can be reached easily by local bus routes or taxi from the city centre, with entry fees that are affordable for individuals and families. The festival's open-air gallery is continuously refreshed by master sculptors from around the world, who shape mythological creatures, historical icons, and pop culture figures out of nothing

but sand and water. It's not just a viewing experience—visitors can take part in sand sculpting workshops, enjoy light shows after dusk, and wander among creations that tower several metres high, lending the beach an almost surreal quality.

Antalya Piano Festival

Taking place in November, the Antalya Piano Festival is an elegant celebration of classical music that draws world-renowned pianists to perform in venues like the Antalya Culture Centre. Situated in the heart of the city, the location is easily reachable by tram, bus, or foot if you're staying nearby. With reasonably priced tickets, the festival invites both connoisseurs and casual listeners to experience the emotive power of piano music in a refined, acoustically rich setting. Since its inception in 2000, the festival has played a crucial role in Turkey's cultural calendar, enhancing Antalya's reputation as more than just a beach destination. Attendees can expect solo recitals, orchestral performances, and masterclasses, all of which serve as a reminder that Antalya's heart beats not only to the rhythm of waves, but also to the resonance of music.

8.2 Antalya Golden Orange Film Festival

The Antalya Golden Orange Film Festival, known locally as "Antalya Altın Portakal Film Festivali," is Turkey's longest-running and most prestigious film celebration. Held every October in the Mediterranean city of Antalya, it draws filmmakers, critics, artists and cinema lovers from across the world. It's a vibrant confluence of culture, cinema and the creative arts, presenting an immersive week of screenings, discussions and red-carpet glamour that transforms the city into Turkey's cinematic heartbeat.

Opening Ceremony at Antalya Culture Center

The festival commences with a grand opening ceremony held at the Antalya Kültür Merkezi (Antalya Culture Center), a revered venue situated in the Muratpaşa district of the city. Attendees can access the venue via tram lines from central Kaleiçi, with no entry fee for those with pre-booked festival passes. The ceremony is a dazzling event showcasing celebrity arrivals, live musical performances and tributes to Turkish cinema legends, setting the emotional and aesthetic tone for the week ahead. It's a rare moment when local tradition and global glamour unite, reaffirming the city's long-standing dedication to cinema since the festival's inception in 1963. Visitors are advised to arrive early, dress smartly, and soak in the electric atmosphere that marks the beginning of a cinematic pilgrimage.

National Feature Film Competition Screenings

A cornerstone of the festival is the National Feature Film Competition, which brings Turkey's finest contemporary films into the spotlight, held mainly in the Nazım Hikmet Cultural Centre and the AKM Aspendos Hall. Screenings take place throughout the week, and access is usually available with a nominal ticket fee or free with accreditation passes. Films are introduced by directors and followed by discussions, allowing for deep engagement with the craft and culture of Turkish cinema. This section is vital for understanding the socio-political fabric of modern Turkey as interpreted through the lens of its filmmakers, making it a richly educational experience for cinephiles. Those planning to attend should consult the official festival program to choose films aligning with their interests and arrive early, as seats fill quickly.

International Film Screenings and Guest Appearances

Held primarily at the Migros AVM Cinetech Cinemas and supplemented by open-air venues across the Konyaaltı beachfront, the international screenings are the festival's window to the world. Featuring acclaimed films from Europe, Asia and the Americas, this event offers Antalya a touch of global sophistication each October. Visitors can buy individual screening tickets or opt for festival bundles, with most films subtitled in English and Turkish. These screenings often feature post-film talks with directors, offering candid insights into the stories behind the lens. It is here that international guests mingle with Turkish audiences, generating cultural dialogue that surpasses borders and showcasing Antalya as not just a tourist destination but a global hub of artistic exchange.

Altın Portakal Sinema Tırı

One of the festival's most cherished traditions is the Altın Portakal Sinema Tırı, a mobile cinema truck that brings the magic of the big screen to the more remote towns and districts surrounding Antalya. Travelling through towns like Serik, Kumluca and Elmalı in the lead-up to the festival, this initiative is offered free to the public, drawing families and rural communities who might otherwise never access such an event. The project bridges the urban-rural divide and reaffirms the festival's mission of inclusivity, ensuring the spirit of cinema touches all corners of Antalya. The mobile screenings are typically Turkish classics or family-friendly dramas, making them ideal for travellers interested in local community culture and grassroots arts initiatives.

Closing Gala and Award Night at Glass Pyramid Sabancı Congress Center

The festival concludes with a glittering closing gala hosted at the Glass Pyramid Sabancı Congress and Exhibition Center, a modern structure situated within the lush grounds of Cam Piramit Park. Accessible via local buses or taxis from the city center, the gala night is invitation-only, though portions are televised and streamed online for broader access. The event includes award presentations for Best Film, Best Director and Audience Choice, often followed by performances and an after-party for industry insiders. For visitors fortunate enough to attend or witness it from outside, it's a moment of celebration that encapsulates a week of artistry, ambition and cultural pride. The legacy of the Altın Portakal awards continues to shape Turkish cinema, making this event not just a finale, but a firm nod to the future.

8.3 Cultural Events and Concerts

Antalya, the cultural heart of Turkey's Mediterranean coast, is more than sun-soaked beaches and ancient ruins—it is a thriving stage for music, dance, and tradition. Throughout the year, the city hosts a rich tapestry of cultural festivals and live concerts that stir the senses and connect past legacies to modern expression. These events do not merely entertain—they serve as open-air classrooms of Anatolian heritage, expressions of national pride, and living reminders of Antalya's artistic soul.

Antalya Piano Festival

Held every November, the Antalya Piano Festival, or "Antalya Piyano Festivali" as it is known locally, brings the city to a melodic crescendo. Entry fees vary by performance but typically begin around 100 TL, with tickets available online or at the venue. Founded in 2000, the festival was initially launched under the guidance of famous Turkish pianist Fazıl Say, whose vision was to elevate Antalya's cultural profile through music. Attending the festival is more than hearing notes—it is witnessing dialogue between East and West, tradition and modernity, in a setting where the applause feels earned and the atmosphere reverent.

Aspendos International Opera and Ballet Festival

Each June, within the timeless grandeur of the 2,000-year-old Aspendos Theatre, the Aspendos Opera and Ballet Festival, or "Aspendos Uluslararası Opera ve Bale Festivali," transforms ancient stone into a living stage. Situated 45 kilometers east of Antalya's city center in the town of Serik, visitors can reach the theatre by intercity buses, taxis, or guided tours departing from Kaleiçi and Lara. Entry fees hover around 300 TL for premium seating, a small price for the grandeur of full-scale operatic and ballet performances echoing in one of the best-preserved Roman theatres in the world. The event, first inaugurated in 1994, holds deep cultural meaning as a testament to Turkey's commitment to classical arts amidst a heritage site of unmatched historic magnitude.

International Antalya Sand Sculpture Festival

Sculptors from across the world descend upon Antalya to create colossal, intricate sand artworks based on rotating themes such as mythology, history, or cinema. Accessible by public buses from Antalya city center and priced around 200 TL for adults, the festival offers a full day's worth of exploration and wonder. Unlike other cultural events, this one invites slow observation, engaging all ages with its ephemeral beauty and craftsmanship. It was first launched in the early 2000s and has grown into one of the most distinctive sand art festivals globally. It appeals to both the casual onlooker and the artistically inclined, making it a rewarding outing for families, solo travelers, and photography enthusiasts alike.

International Antalya Film Festival

With origins tracing back to 1963, this one of Turkey's oldest and most prestigious film events, blending screenings, competitions, and discussions in both local and international categories. Entrance fees range from 50 to 150 TL depending on the screening, with discounted student options available. Easily accessible via tram or public bus from the city center, the festival not only celebrates cinema but also revives public discourse on art, identity, and societal shifts. With its signature Golden Orange Award, the event has launched careers, honored pioneers, and served as a cultural mirror for Turkish society through the decades. For film lovers and curious minds alike, it offers a weeklong immersion into a world of stories.

Antalya International Folk Music and Dance Festival

Known locally as "Antalya Uluslararası Halk Dansları ve Müzik Festivali," Antalya International Folk music is a jubilant celebration of global heritage. Performers from various continents showcase their nations' traditional dances, instruments, and costumes, creating a dazzling mosaic of cultures in harmony. Events often take place in Cumhuriyet Square, Karaalioğlu Park, and public theatres, with free public performances enhancing accessibility for all. The festival is a vibrant, family-friendly event that promotes unity and preserves fading traditions through performance and storytelling. Initiated in the 1990s as part of Turkey's broader cultural diplomacy efforts, it stands today as a cherished event that brings warmth, rhythm, and diversity to Antalya's late summer nights, offering a vibrant atmosphere where one can dance, observe, and be reminded of the world's shared musical roots.

8.4 Traditional Turkish Nights

Antalya, the glittering jewel of Turkey's Mediterranean coast, doesn't merely shine under the sun—it comes alive when the sun sets. For those seeking a deep, evocative immersion into Turkish culture, the city's famed "Turkish Nights" offer evenings that blend folk traditions, Ottoman splendour, and Anatolian storytelling into a living theatre. These nights are far more than just entertainment—they are windows into a nation's soul, filled with music, dance, food, and centuries-old hospitality that continue to define Turkish identity.

Kervansaray Turkish Night at Antalya Kervansaray Hotel

Known locally as "Kervansaray Türk Gecesi," this evening event is held within the atmospheric Kervansaray Hotel in Lara Beach, particularly popular from April through October when the tourist season is in full swing. The hotel's elegant Ottoman-themed courtyard, lit by lanterns and scented with blooming citrus, transforms into a grand stage where dervish dancers twirl in hypnotic unison and belly dancers tell tales without words. Entry typically ranges from 40 to 60 Euros per person, often inclusive of an open buffet of traditional Turkish fare and unlimited local drinks. The cultural draw lies in its carefully choreographed show that recreates Ottoman wedding scenes, henna nights, and nomadic village celebrations, all with live Turkish folk music and masterful instrumentation. Visitors can take part in the communal dances and taste Anatolia's finest dishes, making it not only a night of viewing but one of total participation and memory-making.

Sema Ceremony and Turkish Dinner at Mevlevi Sufi Lodge

Held in the Mevlevihane district of Kaleiçi—the historic heart of Antalya—this spiritual Turkish night is often referred to in the local tongue as the "Sema Gösterisi." This deeply reverent event is more subdued than the tourist-focused alternatives, taking place year-round, but most commonly between March and November, when more visitors flow through the Old Town. The highlight of the evening is the whirling dervish ceremony, a ritual of the Mevlevi Sufis symbolising a spiritual journey through mind and love to divine perfection. It's not a ticketed commercial event but rather an intimate gathering, with donations appreciated in place of a fixed entry fee. After the dervish ceremony, a modest yet authentic Turkish meal is served, often featuring lentil soup, börek, stuffed vine leaves, and strong Turkish tea. For those seeking spiritual depth and cultural enlightenment, this experience offers an unfiltered connection to Turkish mysticism in one of the oldest functioning religious lodges of the region.

Yoruk Tent Turkish Night Experience at Tünektepe Hill

Best visited from May to September, this Turkish Night is held in traditional nomadic-style tents, where the decor features goat hair rugs, low cushions, and wood-fired ovens. For an entrance fee of around 50 Euros, guests are welcomed with sherbet drinks and can savour spit-roasted lamb, flatbread cooked over open flame, and locally produced ayran. Performances are staged by local folk troupes showcasing the fiery dances of the Taurus Mountains, complete with zurna music and drum-accompanied sword dances. Beyond the visual spectacle, it holds cultural value as a tribute to the Yoruk tribes who once roamed these hills with their flocks. The experience is as much about storytelling and ancestral pride as it is about festive celebration, and visitors leave with a tangible understanding of a vanishing nomadic heritage.

Ottoman Palace Turkish Night at Club Aura Kemer

In the lively resort town of Kemer, Club Aura hosts a vibrant Turkish Night known locally as "Osmanlı Sarayı Gecesi." The event blends the glamour of a modern nightclub with stylised depictions of Ottoman imperial pageantry, held regularly from June through October. The show opens with janissary marches, continues through mock palace scenes with sultans and harem dancers, and concludes with spirited belly dancing performances and a communal halay dance where the audience is encouraged to join in. Located just a short drive from central Antalya, shuttle buses are often arranged by tour companies. The entry fee, typically around 60 Euros, includes traditional meze platters and Anatolian grilled mains, plus a selection of raki and wines. Visitors get swept into a past where pageantry and power ruled the Mediterranean shores, all wrapped in a festive, high-energy atmosphere.

Aspendos Turkish Night at Ancient Aspendos Theatre Grounds

This rare event, known as "Aspendos Türk Gecesi," is held occasionally during special cultural festivals such as in June and September and is among the most atmospheric of all. While the ancient Roman theatre itself is too delicate for regular shows, nearby performance spaces and outdoor amphitheatres within the Aspendos archaeological park host these open-air Turkish Nights under the stars. Entry costs range from 50 to 70 Euros, with group rates available, and transportation is often included from Antalya's city centre as the site is located about 45 minutes eastward. It is here that culture, time, and tradition coalesce, offering a Turkish Night that feels both ancient and ever-relevant, designed for the traveler who values authenticity over theatrics.

CONCLUSION AND INSIDER TIPS

There are places that merely occupy space on a map, and then there are places like Antalya that leave their mark on your spirit. As your footprints wash away from the Mediterranean shores, the memories cling to you like the sun on your skin. This guide may end, but your story with Antalya is only just beginning.

A Land Where History and Horizon Meet

Antalya is not one place but many layered over one another—each ancient ruin, sun-drenched harbour, and narrow alley holding whispers of a thousand years past. You walk through it not as a tourist but as a quiet witness to history that still breathes. The city has mastered the delicate balance of past and present, where timeworn relics sit side by side with modern cafés, and tales of empires past echo gently behind each waterfall. It's a place where every turn uncovers something ageless.

People Make the Place—And Antalya's Are Gold

One thing that sets Antalya apart isn't found in a brochure—it's the people. Hospitality here isn't a service; it's an unspoken code. You'll find old men offering you tea in shadowed courtyards, market women pressing fruit into your hands, and hoteliers who treat you as a long-lost relative. These human moments, unscripted and spontaneous, are the true souvenirs of your journey. You will forget the ticket prices and travel times, but you will never forget the kindness.

Off the Beaten Track Is Where the Magic Happens

It's tempting to stay in the known—the beaches, the resorts, the picture-postcard views—but Antalya rewards those who wander deeper. Take the wrong street in Kaleiçi and find yourself in a courtyard that feels like a secret garden. Venture into the sleepy mountain villages and hear a dialect you won't find in phrasebooks. Book a dolmuş just to see where it takes you. These unscheduled adventures are where Antalya's soul reveals itself most honestly.

When to Go Is Up to You, But Every Season Has a Secret

While summer steals the spotlight with its golden beaches and late-night buzz, Antalya holds secrets best unlocked by each season. Spring brings almond blossoms and uncrowded ruins. Autumn paints the hills in deep ochres and rusts, perfect for hikes and quiet strolls. Even in winter, the city slows into something intimate, where locals reclaim the rhythm and fireside tea becomes the main event. There's no wrong time—only the right moment waiting to be discovered.

Essential Wisdom Only Locals Will Tell You

Always carry small cash—street food here is divine, but card machines are rare in the best places. Don't plan every detail; let the unexpected find you. Respect the traditions—modesty is admired, even on the beach. And never, ever turn down a glass of Turkish tea, for in that moment, you're not just a visitor; you've become part of someone's story.

Leaving Antalya isn't an end; it's a change in tempo. The city becomes something you carry—in the way you pause to watch a sunset, in how the smell of spices makes your heart ache a little, in your craving for sea air when land feels too heavy. This guide may close in your hands, but it opens something far greater in your mind. You will return, whether by flight or in memory, because Antalya never really lets go. And deep down, you'll be grateful it doesn't.

Printed in Dunstable, United Kingdom